Life in the S.L.O.W. Lane

An Educator's Guide for Managing Stress and Maintaining Well Being

Lauren Kazee, LMSW

Edited by Joann B. Fisher

THE WRITE AGENT

Life in the S.L.O.W. Lane: An Educator's Guide for Managing Stress and Maintaining Well Being

ISBN 978-0-9801159-2-5
Library of Congress Control Number: 2023902490

THE WRITE AGENT

Publisher
The Write Agent, LLC
3470 McClure Bridge Road
#792
Duluth, GA 30096

AUTHOR

LAUREN KAZEE, LMSW

For over three decades, Lauren Kazee has devoted her career to the welfare of others. She obtained both her Bachelor and Master of Social Work degrees from the University of Illinois, Jane Addams College of Social Work, in 1993 and 1994, respectively.

She is a licensed professional and currently does contract work for many child-serving entities, including the State of Michigan, around staff and student social, emotional, and mental health. She headed the group at MDE to create Michigan's Birth through Grade 12 Social and Emotional Learning (SEL) Competencies, alongside several supporting resources for SEL implementation.

In 2018, Lauren founded her company, Living S.L.O.W. LLC, and has since then supplied keynote sessions, breakouts, and consultancy to hundreds of teachers and other educators, aiding them in prioritizing self-care and accomplishing their goals.

To
My family and inner circle who have driven me to the joy of going S.L.O.W.

Special Thanks to
Educators and Administrators devoted to service.
It's time to give yourself permission to go S.L.O.W.

PREFACE

At 33, I had dwindled down to a mere 110 lbs. Seated on my back porch swing, I observed my two young children playing outside while I considered taking my own life.

My carefully constructed worldview was being shaken. To start, my parents parted ways after almost forty years of marriage. They had been my beacon of hope for marital bliss and the model of a healthy relationship. Furthermore, the religious community I had been part of since I was two years old was in a state of chaos. This organization had been the source of many childhood memories and eventually my place of employment for numerous years. In essence, it had been the foundation of my faith and self-identity. Through all of this, my marriage was crumbling. I felt lost, afraid, and hopeless.

As a trained therapist, I am familiar with the signs of suicidal ideation. In my case, regardless of my training, I knew I needed outside help. Driven by my love for my children, which was much more intense than my love for myself, I sought the assistance that I desperately needed.

I underwent two years of therapy with a highly qualified and reliable professional. With her guidance, I unearthed who I truly was under all the misconceptions others had taught me about myself and the person I was striving to be. She gave me permission to feel my feelings and acknowledge I had needs and that was okay. In the process, I began to unlearn a lifetime of beliefs rooted in the mistaken assumption that prioritizing my own wants and feelings meant I was being selfish and conceited at the expense of others.

To eat or not to eat:

If someone asked me where I wanted to eat, I would always defer to others, never feeling like it was ok to say what I wanted or needed (which is always Mexican)

PREFACE

I can still recall these arguments with my husband where he would invariably say, "Just tell me what you need."

I would respond with exasperation, "I don't know."

Sadly, that was the God's honest truth. I genuinely had no clue. I could list the things I was supposed to need or feel, but in reality, I was like a robot – disconnected and afraid of doing something wrong.

Embracing the freedom to feel and need and want has taken time and requires constant practice. In fact, I'm still learning. It has been and remains a process that enables me to evolve, perhaps even mature, into the woman I am becoming and have always wanted to be - strong, competent, self-assured, kind, gracious, loving, and fun. Even my children can vouch that I've finally become "fun" after all these years.

During my therapeutic journey, there were a number of noteworthy moments. One particular session served as a tipping point for what I share in this workbook. My Living S.L.O.W. philosophy is my call to educators, administrators and anyone in a caregiving profession to retrain their thinking and embrace the values and benefits of practicing self-care.

I designed this workbook after considering the needs of the hundreds of educators and individuals who attend my workshops seeking answers on how to be the best version of themselves in their field. So, turn on your indicator, move over to the right lane, and let's take it S.L.O.W.

Self-care strategies:

- Require forethought
- Require planning
- Require commitment
- Require action

INTRODUCTION

I was discussing an incident that occurred one day while working at the Department of Education with my therapist. In my role as the School Mental Health Consultant, I was composing an annual report for a federal grant given to our state. While collecting the data to send, I remembered I hadn't told the budget analyst that I needed the financial status report, which best practice asks we give her two weeks to generate.

Working for the government is always a slow process, and in this case, my Type A personality brought on a serious case of anxiety. Yet, she got me what I needed immediately, so all should have been right with the world. Unfortunately, despite my colleague's generosity in providing what I needed right away, I still felt the need to apologize continuously, brooding over the error I had made, even though she had already forgiven me.

It was on this issue that my therapist enlightened me. My constant apologizing took up more time than necessary and distracted those around me, including myself. She had done me a favor, but I couldn't see beyond my mistake. Had I given myself some grace, I could have released the guilt and moved on.

Ironically, my therapist sent me home with the acronym "F.A.S.T.," which, honestly, I can't recall it's meaning outside of the "A" - Apologize once!

The effect of the acronym F.A.S.T. lingered for a few days, but gradually it began to register. The more I reminded myself to "Go F.A.S.T.," the more out of sorts I felt. F.A.S.T. made me feel like I had to rush even more to keep up. The acronym, which was designed to help me let go and move forward, ended up intensifying my anxiety and energy levels.

That's when I changed F.A.S.T. to S.L.O.W.

That one change from F.A.S.T. to S.L.O.W. reminded me to:
- Pace myself
- Be more aware
- Simply take a breath

In that moment, as my pulse slowed and my spirit calmed, I found myself on the other side of my ever-pressing anxieties. On both a personal and professional level, I was moving from darkness to light. That's how I got here, and that's how S.L.O.W. was born.

This tumultuous period, alongside a string of epiphanies, forced me to intentionally slow down, decelerate if you will, and moderate the pace at which I was going through life. It made me conscious of my needs and prompted me to actively engage in the preservation of my well-being.

I have learned to intuit the signs of my own burn-out–impatience, sarcasm, crabbiness. In those moments, my fuse is short, and I have no tolerance for anything. That is not the core of my identity; I want to represent the authentic "me." S.L.O.W. helped me to get there.

In this workbook, I share the lessons from 2017 through 2021 and cluster them by month. I structure them in this way to allow you, the reader, to follow along over the course of a school year. I tailor the lessons to address the potential happenings related to that timeframe. So, for example, January lessons may refer to coming back after the holiday break. June lessons may allude to preparing for summer break, and so on. I also broken them up into four seasons, but not the typical seasons. Here I divided them into the "Back to School" season, the "Whimsical Winter" season, the "Spring to the Finish Line" season and finally, "Slide into Summer" season. This format allows you to select the season in which you find yourself, and start from there. Ultimately, however, do what works best for you!

TABLE OF CONTENTS

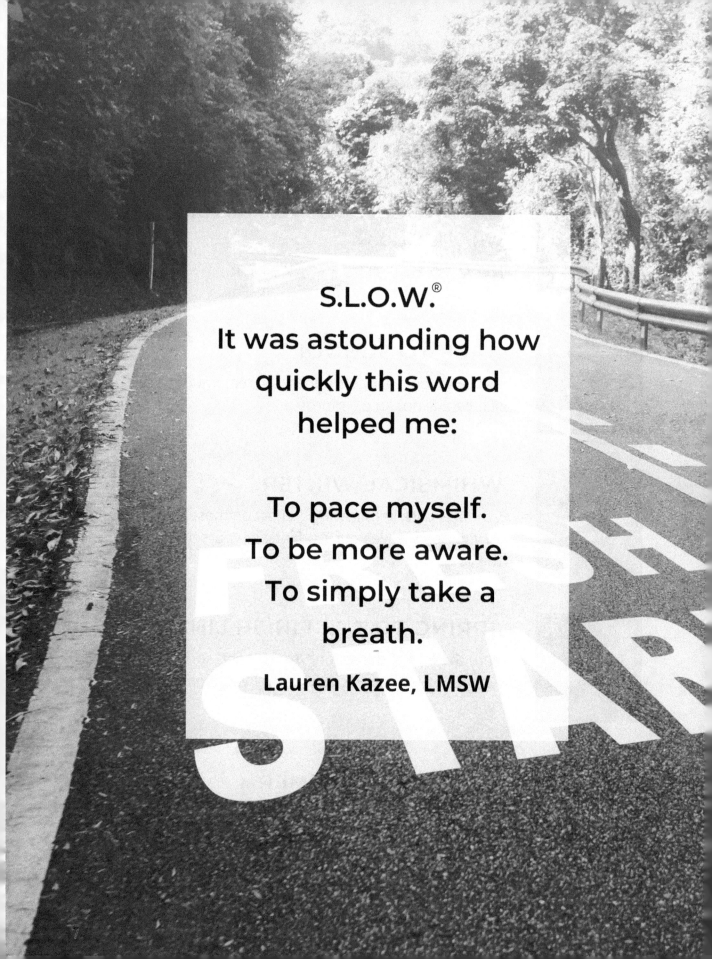

S.L.O.W.®
It was astounding how quickly this word helped me:

To pace myself.
To be more aware.
To simply take a breath.

Lauren Kazee, LMSW

PART

living
S.L.O.W.™

1

AN EDUCATOR'S GUIDE FOR
MANAGING STRESS AND MAINTAINING WELL-BEING

<u>WHAT YOU'LL GET FROM THIS BOOK</u>

As a mental health professional, I know that self-care is an essential part of life. Educators and administrators found it particularly challenging to adjust to the sudden changes to their work environment.

Covid-19 pushed many of us beyond already challenging mental limits, and it became more evident that educators needed a resource to enhance their skills around their well-being.

This book compendium of revised monthly blogs published to the Living S.L.O.W. website, along with newly added reflection activities, is intended to help in that process. The philosophy behind Living S.L.O.W. is that small, easily embedded daily actions can bolster wellness for educators anywhere.

<u>CORE CONCEPTS</u>

You will learn to:
- Prioritize your well being
- Manage out of control stress levels
- Improve self-awareness
- Integrate self-care into daily life without sacrificing your passion as an educator

WHAT IS S.L.O.W.?

S

STICK TO YOUR VALUES

In contrast to F.A.S.T., the idea behind S.L.O.W. may resonate more with you. The values of family, health, friends, integrity, and nature top the list for most people. But, how often do you neglect these values in favor of work obligations? By prioritizing the things you value most, you remain close to your identity and authenticity, which in turn boosts your health.

L

LOVE YOURSELF FIRST, THEN OTHERS

It's difficult to prioritize yourself over loved ones, given your propensity to nurture as an educator. In this field, selflessness is an essential element. However, if you don't take care of yourself, what can you bring to the table for others? Do you often go from task to task without rest? If you're running on fumes, it will weigh heavily on your emotional state.

O

ONLY APOLOGIZE ONCE

Constantly apologizing appears positive as it shows ownership of your behavior. However, I must emphasize that one sincere and humble apology should be enough. Don't let one mistake dictate your emotions. There is no need to apologize multiple times to demonstrate contrition. Acknowledge your misstep, release it, and embrace grace even it's only from you.

W

WATCH AND WAIT

This strategy is a must whether on purpose or because there's no alternative. I don't typically relinquish control so that chaos might reign. That's not where this is going. But, allowing things to naturally unfold without interference can be fun. Granted, "going with the flow" has its own drawbacks. But, are you willing to let go if it means protecting your peace?

S.L.O.W.
**A simple acronym that changed the way I now choose to navigate life.
Use this workbook to see where it can take you!**

HOW TO USE THIS WORKBOOK

STEP

Before each season, take an assessment. This helps put you in touch with where you've been and how prepared you are for what comes next. It helps you preview where you can fit in self-care strategies

STEP

Read each post then complete the exercises that follow. There are 5 exercises with each section. If additional journaling is needed, please use the note pages at the back of the book.

STEP

Complete the S.L.O.W. **review** at the end of each Quarter. Then, complete the S.L.O.W. quarterly **preview** to prepare for the upcoming season.

PART

living
S.L.O.W.™

2

BACK TO SCHOOL

Starting with the "Back to School" season is intentional. Arguably, this can be the most topsy-turvy time of the school year. You spend a lot of time getting back into the swing of things while establishing relationships with new students, their families, and possibly new colleagues. To say that there are endless opportunities to neglect self-care would be an understatement. It's important to pace yourself, so this workbook begins with this time of year in hopes you'll establish healthy habits right out of the gate.

AUGUST
- You have the Power
- Be Calm
- Good Enough is Good Enough
- Slow and Steady Wins the Race
- Problem Solving

SEPTEMBER
- Back to School Supplies
- New Beginnings
- Just One More Thing
- You Might as Well
- Ignorance is Bliss

OCTOBER
- Our Perception is Our Reality
- Wasting Time Away
- Reframe Game
- Pace Yourself
- Hard But Not Impossible

First: Complete the assessment on the following page.

FALL ASSESSMENT

		YES	NO
1	At the beginning of the school year, I have a renewed sense of anticipation for all the new school year will bring.	☐	☐
2	By the time school starts, I have already planned out the year ahead, including time to deal with unexpected chaos.	☐	☐
3	I have healthy work habits that can hopefully offset the the impact of work strains that inevitably lie ahead.	☐	☐
4	It's easy for me to get caught up in the "routine of life" and forget to prioritize self-care activities throughout the day.	☐	☐
5	For this quarter, I have already identified readily available opportunities for self-care.	☐	☐
6	My mindset about the fall season definitely impacts my emotions, outlook, attitude, and actions.	☐	☐
7	I have go-to activities that prepare me to handle situations I may encounter during this time of year.	☐	☐
8	I usually maintain a positive outlook this time of year on work, my students, and my colleagues.	☐	☐

NOTES

NOTES

AUGUST

August is an interesting month because it's still summer but as the month proceeds, we head into a new school year. You can sense the wheels of life churn faster and faster as things ramp back up. I do a lot of professional development for educators, so this is typically a very busy month for me.

As tiresome as it can be traveling from place to place, I absolutely LOVE my time spent with educators. They are some of my favorite people as they are resilient and hopeful even during hard times. There is a renewed sense of anticipation for all the new school year will bring.

I appreciate having time with school staff before things are in full force, as I hope to help reinforce healthy habits that might offset the impact of work strains that inevitably lie ahead. The August lessons are good reminders that we can control how we respond to the rat race.

As we head into a new school year, we get to determine our speed and our degree of investment. We can run helter-skelter and only accept perfection from ourselves, or we can pace ourselves and do our best. In my opinion, the latter option is perfection!

You Have the Power

My birthday is in June, and I took the day off from work. I grabbed some fruit, nuts, water, and a blanket, then enjoyed the sizzling outdoors (I made a beeline for shaded areas) in solitude at the botanical gardens reading the new book from one of my favorite authors. Like many, I also reflected on my life, the last year, and the future I desire.

Even though that day evokes introspection, I hope people don't just wait until their birthday to reflect. Life gives you various opportunities to stop and think about where you are, where you are going and even where you want to go.

Each new year is another time of contemplation and resolution.

As educators, the start of a new school year is an opportunity to not only organize curricula, decorations, and classrooms but also to assess your own mindset as you embark upon the fresh year and all the possibilities that come along with it. Subsequently, you do not need conventional occasions for self-reflection and direction. In fact, each new day provides the chance to determine your path and next steps.

I spend a lot of time in my car, driving to various meetings, trainings, and conferences across the state I live in. This gives me time to be reflective. Other times, I enjoy taking a walk or running as they are a healthy distraction. What are some things you currently use or could begin to use to start writing your next chapter?

Though I've heard it many times before, only recently did it click that I get to define and control the direction of my life. I'm actually embarrassed to admit that. But I know it's not just true for me. Is it true for you too? You have the power to write your story. You are in control of the pages and chapters of your life's story.

REFLECTIONS

1) When have you felt the most powerful?

_____
_____
_____
_____
_____
_____

2) When have you felt the most powerless?

_____
_____
_____
_____
_____
_____

3) What was different in each scenario that caused a different outcome?

_____
_____
_____
_____
_____
_____

4) What can you use to feel powerful more frequently?

_____
_____
_____
_____
_____
_____

Be CALM

At the start of this school year, a shift in my life circumstances forced me to do a lot of soul-searching, introspection, and reflection. Some days, I peacefully embraced self-care, practiced what I preached, and lived S.L.O.W.. Other days, I was uptight, anxious, short-fused and difficult to be around. Simply put, I sucked at living S.L.O.W.! Needless to say, I doubted my ability to provide sound advice to anyone on taking care of themselves. However, I realized that being vulnerable about the real struggles we encounter when trying to prioritize self-care is necessary, even essential!

There was one week when I could hardly sleep. As adrenaline surged through my body, my mind and emotions were running at full speed. I tried unsuccessfully to relax by reading, meditating, enjoying soaking baths and more. Nothing worked. One night before I went to bed, I texted my struggles to my son.

He said, "try to be patient, present and peaceful. Control your emotions and calm your mind as best as you can." Wow! Be patient, present, peaceful. Be controlled and calm. I wrote "calm" on the notepad beside my bed and each night, I look at that word and think, Be CALM. Seeing that word as I end my day helps. It reminds me to be patient and gracious with myself and to stay present in knowing all is well and all will be well.

These hectic life changes have not only forced me to incorporate self-care strategies, but they make me appreciate teachers and other professionals who are pulled in a thousand directions all day.

As you reflect on how to maximize brief moments of time, here are a few ideas to help you get started:
- Take a moment to laugh, watch a funny video, or hug a loved one
- Name 2 things you are grateful for
- Close your eyes for three minutes and be present and at peace

Take a breath and calm your emotions

REFLECTIONS

IF YOU WERE TO CHANGE CALM INTO AN ACRONYM, WHAT WOULD THE "C" REPRESENT FOR YOU?

A. CONFIDENT   C. CAREFUL
B. CAREFREE   D OTHER_____

SOMETIMES, ALL IT TAKES IS ONE WORD TO BRING YOU PEACE OF MIND. IDENTIFY FOUR WORDS, THEN CIRCLE YOUR MOST PEACEFUL WORD.

A. _____   C. _____
B. _____   D _____

HOW OFTEN DO YOU PRIORITIZE SELF-CARE EACH WEEK? HOW OFTEN CAN YOU?

A. ONCE   C. 5 TIMES
B. 3 TIMES   D NEVER

WHAT SELF-CARE ACTIVITIES CAN YOU FIT IN TO BRIEF MOMENTS THROUGHOUT YOUR DAY?

A. _____   C. _____
B. _____   D _____

Good Enough is Good Enough

In the past, summer usually brought about a slower pace, a time to kick back a little, relax and refuel. However, this year it seems as if the pace hasn't slowed and there is more pressure to "get things done."

Recently, before a meeting on Social Emotional Learning (SEL), I asked a coworker how she was doing. Her answer was simply, "stressed." As we discussed further, she and I realized that while we appreciate and are committed to high-quality work, sometimes it's ok that what we do at work can be "good enough."

First, it takes time and practice to build that "it's good enough" muscle, recognizing what will and what won't produce effectively better work. While there are some things that demand and require our highest abilities, fullest attention, and best work, not everything has to be "the best" or "perfect."

Second, it also takes time and practice to surrender to this mindset and to actually "move on" - whether at work or in your day-to-day life. Sometimes we can be our own worst enemy. More often than not, WE are the ones instilling that expectation, not those in our home or work circles. My internal need to look good to those around me was the driving force. I was stressing myself out with unnecessary expectations.

It's important to be mindful of what is realistic to expect from yourself and others, and to learn to surrender that need to look or be perfect. Don't miss out on the light-hearted, free, or enjoyable moments that present themselves throughout your day. There's a saying "stop and smell the roses," but are you more focused on pulling the weeds?

As you begin to wind down your summer and think about a new school year, are there things you can put in the "good enough" category? Can your seating chart or bulletin board be good enough? What things truly need your best effort? My hope is you can begin a new school year refreshed and committed to taking care of yourself.

REFLECTIONS

Would you or others say you're a perfectionist? If yes, what's the motivation behind it? Who or what do you impact with this trait? If things aren't "good enough," do you or others notice?

_____
_____
_____
_____
_____
_____
_____

It's hard to let go of expectations for high-quality products or performance. Be intentional about ways you can release some "perfect" pressure as you go about your day. Other thoughts and takeaways from this lesson:

_____
_____
_____
_____
_____
_____
_____
_____
_____
_____
_____

Slow and Steady Wins the Race

I really wrestled with what the lesson should be for this month. The 2020 pandemic left a lot of consternation around "returning to learn," and students, educators, and families were under a lot of stress. Could everyone adhere to safety measures if in person instruction occurred? Even though those days are now behind us, they afforded an opportunity to prioritize self-care.

Today, it's no different. It's essential to keep self-care at the top of your list, even during a busy time, to avoid getting caught up in the noise and stress. I set boundaries with my schedule and prioritize self-care activities, such as taking breaks, walking the dog, or even taking a power nap.

It can be difficult to do that while racing through the day. There are requests, deadlines, and emails in addition to our own personal anxiety about the unknown future. However, it's important to learn new strategies to ensure that you go S.L.O.W. and steady yourself while the world spins around you.

Be intentional about how many meetings you schedule in a day or, if you have an unusually full day, seek ways to lighten the load for the next day.

Finally, practice self-care by staying in your lane. I came to realize I don't always have to "fix" everything and neither do you. Stay quiet and let others do some problem solving. You don't always have to insert yourself as sometimes, it's good to let others take the lead so they, too, can learn something new.

REFLECTIONS

Read the below statements and check the ones that apply to you. Write additional thoughts in the notes section below.

- I have mixed feelings about letting others take on responsibilities.

- I am concerned about my students' and colleagues' mental health and well-being.

- As a means of self-care, I think it's important to step away from social media.

- I set boundaries and schedules that help me prioritize self-care.

- When it comes to leadership roles, I think it's important to stay in my lane.

- I have a list of self-care activities I can incorporate into my day.

Notes:
_____
_____
_____
_____

Problem Solving

During the onset of the COVID-19 pandemic and the subsequent lockdown, puzzle making was all the rage. I engaged in the craze, challenging myself to 1000-piece puzzles and even established a Puzzles During COVID Facebook page.

It was fun seeing people locally and nationally post their completed works of art. I like the challenge of "puzzling," and savor the ultimate completion of the finished product. Puzzle solving and problem-solving share similar skill sets. They both require putting "pieces" together and breaking down larger issues into smaller pieces one step at a time. Some problems can be as small as finding a mutual meeting time for a small group of people. Other times, they can be larger, like how to fix the education system.

Word on the street is there is no shortage of problems in our schools. If you stop too long and take it all in, it can feel daunting. In this field, we can't wish problems away. Here are some important questions you can ask yourself:

- Do you have a reputation for being a "fixer?"
- Do problems find their way to your email inbox?
- Have you started feeling frustrated, overwhelmed, tired, even irritated when someone brings a problem to you.

If the answer is yes to any of these questions, then it's time for a change.

I learned to change the way I communicate, so now, I say "Hmm. That is a problem. Let's see if we can solve this together." Not only does it validate the problem, but it encourages collegiality and collaboration to work it out. This will ease some stress, as you won't have to carry the "weight" all by yourself.

As you prepare for a new school year, take problems piece by piece, working together with those around you to solve the puzzle. Think about how beautiful it can be as it all comes together.

REFLECTIONS

Reflect on a time that you were faced with a daunting problem, either at work or in your personal life.

What was the problem?

_____

_____

_____

_____

1) What was your role in the scenario?

   ○ Participant   ○ Mentor

   ○ Fixer

2) Were others involved to help resolve the issue?

   ○ Yes, they offered ideas   ○ No, no one helped

   ○ Yes they helped me solve the problem

3) Who developed the problem solving strategy?

   ○ I did   ○ Collaborative effort

   ○ A different co-worker

S.L.O.W. ROAD RULES

AFFIRM YOUR POWER

I use affirmations and other trinkets to tap into my power as needed. Some days I do better than others. We each have the power to change our lives. Commit to owning your power. Determine to use it for good each day, whether for yourself or someone else.

"PERFECT" IS A WASTE OF TIME

It's hard to let go of expectations for high-quality products or performance. And sometimes you shouldn't but sometimes you should. Be intentional about ways you can cut corners. Think about ways you can release some "perfect" pressure off your shoulders as you go throughout your day.

FINISH STRONG

Crossing a finish line or winning at some competition is a great feeling because you know all your hard work, practice, and planning has paid off. Pace yourself as you work to finish what you started. Then relish in that great sense of accomplishment!

WHAT'S THE PROBLEM?

Life can throw curveballs, can't it? It's overwhelming to address all the problems that surface. In the future, consider ways to break them into manageable increments. Give some of those pieces to others and reduce your load.

ONE WORD

Remember, all it takes is one word to help bring you peace of mind. What is your word?

ONE SELF-LOVE RULE

Write one of your self-love rules.

SEPTEMBER

By the time September begins, the school schedule is often rolling full steam ahead. Everyone is finding their groove and getting into the rhythm of the day. This is a busy time!

It's easy to get caught up in the "routine of life" as my dad calls it. Thus, self-care may not come easy for some. Of course, there is also the ongoing legitimate concern of when to fit it in? Who has time for self-care? I agree that no educator, or any other youth-serving professional, has extra time on their hands.

Ideally, societal rules would permit built in self-care structures. However, that is not the educational community we live in. Therefore, my solution is to integrate self-care strategies throughout your day. There are readily available opportunities for self-care during our fast-paced lives if we just seek them.

Ideally, it would be great to have chunks of time, but since that's unlikely, find and utilize smaller moments as they can be just as impactful. Look for those morsels of time in between classes or while going from one place to another. Making mental health management an active part of your day may be easier than you think!

Back to School Supplies

I have mixed feelings about "Back to School." I hate the end of summer, since it's my favorite season. I love the long, warm, carefree days, where there's no homework, lunches to pack, or bedtimes to police. But I also like the excitement of a new school year and all that comes with it:

- the regularity of a schedule
- the sense of the school community
- extra-curricular activities
- the introduction of new material and learnings

It's also fun to get new school supplies. I remember as a little girl being so excited to get a new backpack and lunchbox. I had the same excitement as a mom getting supplies for my kids each year.

Besides getting all our materials and supplies ready, which is necessary in preparing for the new school year, I also think about what else we need to help us be successful. Are we emotionally and mentally ready for the new year? Do we have those kinds of "school supplies" ready and packed into our school bag? What are some things you need to help you have a year that is balanced, healthy and self-protective vs exhausting and stressful?

Let's look at our self-care supply list:
- **Planners** - Think ahead - what can you comfortably commit yourself to?
- **Highlighters** - What strengths can you highlight and build on this year?
- **Ruler** - Measure how much energy you have to expend this year and on what
- **Post Its** - Consider affirmations you can post as reminders of your greatness.
- **Erasers** - What do you need to let go of and erase from your memory?

There may be other items you could include on this list, and I hope you do. I hope you acquire a positive perspective, see your value and worth, and prioritize your needs and wants as you head into a new school year.

REFLECTIONS

WHICH SCHOOL SUPPLIES RESONATE WITH YOU MOST?

A. PLANNER
B. HIGHLIGHTER

C. POST-ITS
D   OTHER_____

WHAT SUPPLIES DO YOU ALREADY HAVE PACKED FOR THIS YEAR?

A. _____
B. _____

C. _____
D   _____

HOW OFTEN DO YOU NEED TO STOCK UP ON SUPPLIES EACH MONTH?

A. ONCE
B. 3 TIMES

C. 5 TIMES
D   NEVER

ARE THERE OTHER SUPPLIES YOU NEED THAT ARE NOT LISTED?

A. _____
B. _____

C. _____
D   _____

New Beginnings

Summer has ended and a new school year is beginning. As much as I dread the end of summer and all the hustle and bustle of a new school year, there is also a bit of excitement and anticipation about all that lies ahead. We experience new students/teachers, clean classrooms, updated materials and supplies and a fresh start, a new beginning.

August is a busy time of year for me professionally, as I am hired by various districts to provide professional development for their staff as they head "back to school." There is a buzz in the air as school staff come back from a time of reprieve. Administrators are ready to instill their vision to their staff, who then take it and run with it. I love how palatable the feeling of hope is in those moments.

Starting anything new can be both thrilling and unnerving. If you are anything like me, you need a plan. However, if you're not careful, too much preparation can lead to stress and failure to take in, enjoy and savor the promise of the journey. So, besides focusing on the incoming students, this is also a time to focus on you. Are there ways you can set up your classroom to ensure a calm, positive, supportive environment for not only your students but yourself?

This is a good time to put self-care reminders around the room. Use a coping card or a trinket or both to help you remember your well-being is just as important as the students. Do you have a plan for how you can embed self-care into your daily routine?

A fresh start brings the promise of a better tomorrow. Students and colleagues appreciate starting with a clean slate. Perhaps this year, as classes begin, you can commit to going S.L.O.W.: Stick to our values; Love yourself first, then others around us; Only apologize once; and Wait and Watch. Make your plans, do what you can, but then let it go. Commit to go S.L.O.W., intentionally holding on to the hope of good things to come and believing things work out exactly as they should for your best benefit. Have a great school year!

REFLECTIONS

1)Do you like fresh starts? Why?

_____
_____
_____
_____
_____

2) What's your favorite thing about a new beginning?

_____
_____
_____
_____
_____

3) What goals have you set for yourself this year?

_____
_____
_____
_____
_____

4) Do you see any downsides to new beginnings? If so, how can you overcome them?

_____
_____
_____
_____
_____

Just One More Thing and One Less Thing

One year, I had a medical procedure in July and was feeling fine after a couple of days. My mom cautioned me to rest, but I ignored her and did things nevertheless. My reply to her each time was, "I'm going to do just one more thing, then I will." I think we all have this habit of overdoing it and doing one more thing before we rest, but it usually hurts more than it helps, which was exactly what happened to me since I failed to heed my mother's warnings.

Additionally, I am realizing, there is ALWAYS "one more thing" to do. The list of "to do's" never ends. Back to school can be stressful, especially as teachers begin preparing their classrooms and buying supplies. Some teachers feel excited and others are exhausted, but it is all part of the process. I'm sure there is a bit of that in everyone as they embark on a new school year: excitement, anticipation and a little dread or exhaustion as they get "back to reality."

The intention behind Living S.L.O.W. is to help educators become more aware of simple ways to incorporate self-care into their busy lives. Since we are all very good at pushing through and doing "one more thing," my hope is we can shift that perspective and look for ways to do "one LESS thing."

I got sick after overdoing it physically, which forced me to evaluate my to-do list and identify what I could exclude, delegate, or wait on (the "w" in S.L.O.W.). I was conscious about finding one less thing to do. At the end of the day, it was liberating to realize I didn't have to overdo it or push myself.

I'm feeling better these days and back to my regularly scheduled life, but I am more aware of how I pace myself and structure my time. I'm intentional about finding and removing one thing from my daily tasks as often as I can.

My encouragement to you is this. As you begin a new school year or even just a new month, consciously seek ways to lighten your load. Instead of doing "one more thing," find "one less thing" to do. Let your *one more thing* be identifying *one LESS thing* you can do today for yourself. Take care of you!

REFLECTIONS

Make a list of all the things you need to do today (or this week).
Now review that list: Are there things that can wait until
tomorrow/next week? Is there anything you can delegate?

_____

_____

_____

_____

_____

_____

_____

_____

What is the level of urgency for those items? Can you re-prioritize
any of them? Can you distribute them equally over a longer
period of time? Can you consolidate any?

_____

_____

_____

_____

_____

_____

_____

_____

_____

_____

_____

You Might as Well

Lately, it seems my body won't allow me to sleep through the night. Either my bladder needs attention, my temperature won't regulate, my entire body's stiff, or my mind runs nonstop. Needless to say, I don't feel rested and ready to face the next day. As such, on the nights that I get a full rest, I feel like a new woman.

Even though I am writing this lesson after a full 8.5 hours of rest, it seems like everyone is tired! Though the COVID-19 pandemic kept us at home physically, it also took an emotional toll. The new way of working, compounded by the strain of an ongoing pandemic, social unrest, and political and economic tensions, is a lot to shoulder. For any of us, just one of those issues would be a lot to manage.

At a conference where I was a co-presenter to a group of school and district administrators on the need to prioritize their own self-care, the number of attendees pleasantly surprised me. The turnout re-emphasized how much people need reminders for self-care. It was great to process with them and validate the things they are already doing to take care of themselves. We brainstormed new ways to integrate self-care into their busy days and gave them permission and support to recommit to their own well-being.

What's become clearer to me during these various conversations about self-care is that it takes energy. It's hard to prioritize your own needs, but it is necessary. You have to be courageous, stand your ground, and be conscious of your choices.

How I see it is, since you need to spend your energy anyway, *you might as well spend it on yourself*. When you put your needs first, you are then healthy and whole enough to support others. You can't pour from an empty cup. When you fill your cup, it's easier to share your supply. The result is worth it, every time.

REFLECTIONS

Think about all the things on which you spend your energy. Write them down.

Where do I expend my energy?
_____
_____
_____
_____

1) What things build you up?

⬤ ---------------   ⬤ ---------------

⬤ ---------------   ⬤ ---------------

2) What things frustrate you?

⬤ Emails / Meetings   ⬤ Household chores

⬤ Errands   ⬤ Classroom interruptions

3) What can you give your energy to instead?

⬤ ---------------   ⬤ ---------------

⬤ ---------------   ⬤ ---------------

Ignorance is Bliss

At a conference in Michigan's Upper Peninsula, I discussed self-care practices with teachers and administrators from various districts as they prepare for back to school. I also expanded my circle to non-educators and shared self-care tips with employees of a county health department down state in Michigan. Though the job responsibilities of those professionals differ, the level of stress experienced is quite similar. While these events were engaging, it was challenging being on the road and away from the office.

Work life doesn't stop just because you are out in the field. Emails pile up quickly and I was responsible for a training event while traveling, but colleagues graciously covered for me. Despite trying to stay connected, my usual level of control was not possible. As a recovering control freak, it was hard to allow others to take over. I struggled with thoughts of burdening others or not living up to my responsibilities, but realized it was my ego talking. It was important to trust my colleagues and not second-guess my decision to delegate. There is something to be said for staying out of the know, sometimes. I've often said to my adult children, the less I know, the better.

Now granted, I am a social worker, so I care about people and their well-being. However, I also often joke that I became a social worker so I could be in everyone's business and get paid for it. If I am to be mentally healthy, I choose to reserve my energy and brain capacity for things that are important, that need my focus. I check myself by asking:

- Do I really need to be involved in this situation?
- Am I a decision-maker here?
- Is someone else better suited for this circumstance?
- Is there a legitimate reason I need to insert myself?

In many of these cases, the answer is no; I don't need to be included or involved. In those situations, my ignorance is bliss. As I spent hours with educators and other health care professionals, I wanted to know everything, especially about particular students or families we worked with. My encouragement is to go slow - check in with yourself. Do you really need to know? Will it help you help them, or will it cause you to spend energy you could use elsewhere, like on your own well-being? Sometimes, the world needs you to be in it all. Other times, all will be well if you are away.

REFLECTIONS

Read the below statements and check the ones that apply to you.

- I feel liberated when I'm away from work.

- I can fully and completely check out when I'm away from work.

- I worry things at work will fall apart when I'm absent.

- I'm usually disappointed when I return to work.

- Others step up and effectively stand in the gap for me.

- No one steps up and fills my shoes when I'm absent.

Notes:

_____

_____

_____

_____

S.L.O.W. ROAD RULES

REFILL YOUR "SUPPLIES"

Sometimes our supplies run low. Pay attention to when yours need a refill. Get new ones before the old ones run out. Take an inventory of what you have and see what you need. Be prepared to replenish your self-care supplies and be the best you can be this school year.

START FRESH

Fresh beginnings can bring new hope and anticipation. It can also bring stress along with the sense of the unknown. Taking things one step at a time can help. Going SLOW is an option. Think about today and what you need for today. Then do that again tomorrow and the next day. Simply put, start fresh each day.

MORE OR LESS

As amazing as you are, some things will be ok without your input or influence. Don't be your own worse enemy. Notice your own "to do" list and see what you can eliminate. Then check how you respond when you do.

YOU DESERVE IT!

Some things that receive your energy are essential, but so is your well-being and health. Consider ways to receive rather than release more energy. It is important to save and expand energy on things for you! You deserve it!

IGNORANCE AND BLISS

Sometimes it's hard to step back and let others step up because you may not feel as needed. Some find value in always being in the know, but that can be draining. Look for those patterns with yourself. See if you are ok to move to "need to know" only status. Notice if that helps your energy level.

ONE SELF-LOVE RULE

Write one of your self-love rules.

_____

_____

_____

_____

_____

OCTOBER

Most of the people in my life love the fall and everything that comes with the month of October. They love the crispness in the air and "sweater weather." They love the changing leaves and all the colors autumn brings. And so many of them love college football.

I'm ok with all those things, but every year I say, "I would love fall if winter didn't come afterwards." Now if spring came after fall, then I'd be all in!

It's all about perspective. Everyone has their own opinion and point of view. And thus, we behave according to our stance. Our actions follow our beliefs. So, if my attitude is "fall stinks," then I will be crabby while crunching around on the fallen multi-colored leaves, wearing a sweater, on my way to an NCAA game unlike my friends who would be the complete opposite.

It's amazing how our mindset can influence our emotions, outlook, attitude, and actions. Similarly, your outlook on the school year, or your students, or whatever it is you are facing, can make a difference in how it affects you. The October lessons explore this philosophy further.

Our Perception is Our Reality

I was almost home after a long drive from a two-day conference when I hit traffic because of an accident ahead. Rather than be grumpy, I chose to make the most of it. I found an "old school" CD, rolled down the windows, and sung along to every song on that album. As we drove slowly, I chose to feel grateful for many things, including not being in the accident myself and having snacks and water. I also felt empathy for a woman with a toddler in the car next to me. Then it hit me. This unexpected delay was a great chance for some self-care.

As the new school year gets underway, things get busy for me, with lots of travel and conference presentations. I imagine things are busy for you too. Making self-care a priority, even if it's just a few moments, is important.

As rough as things can get in our day to day, ask yourself these questions:
- Where can I see any good?
- Where can I find a highlight?
- What can I count as a blessing?
- Where do you see a silver lining?

Our perception is our reality, so if we perceive that something is the worst thing that could happen, then it may just become that. Changing your perspective is part of self-care and can help us store energy rather than spend it on the negative. One of my favorite quotes for those "rough days" is "well, we can only go up from here." When you look at your students, classroom or school environment, where do you see the good and what can you be grateful for?

That day, I eventually made it home, exhausted but happy and armed with a new perspective. Whether it's being stuck in traffic, a delay at the doctor's office, or a long line at the grocery store, find the silver lining. Reflect on good things, or rock on to your favorite songs. Remember, the situation could be worse than it is, so focus on the opportunities to feed your soul. They are all around you.

REFLECTIONS

Think about a time you felt stuck, either physically or emotionally. Where were you? What was happening around you? Besides feeling stuck, what else did you feel? Anger? Worry? Fear?

_____
_____
_____
_____
_____
_____
_____

What did you do to get unstuck? How did you respond in that situation? Did it work for you? What would you do better next time?

_____
_____
_____
_____
_____
_____
_____
_____
_____
_____

Wasting Time Away

Do you ever say any of these common phrases?:
- "If I can just get through this week."
- "If I can make it to Friday."
- "I can't wait till.... the weekend, or the end of this semester, or the next break."

I know I am definitely guilty of wishing time away. However, as I have caught myself saying some of those phrases above, I've been reconsidering their benefit and can see two sides.

On the one hand, it is helpful to be forward thinking. It gives me hope to look ahead and realize that things won't always be difficult. Likewise, it is also beneficial for me to look back and see where I've been and what I've overcome before. That approach of drawing on successfully navigated previous challenges can also be inspiring, reassuring, and confidence-building.

On the other hand, there is a different side. If we are consistently looking ahead or behind, then we are not present. The older I get, the faster time goes. Because of that, I'm finding that I cherish time more now that I did in my younger years. I've heard my elders say, "Don't wish time away." Now, I get it!

Even though it helps me to think about the future, it also takes me away from relishing or learning in the moment. Even as I sit here at the DMW, I am intentionally trying to make the most of the experience by using the "extra" time to do things I love.

I hope that as you are now knee-deep in a new school year that you remain mindful of making time for yourself, investing in your well-being, and taking advantage of the opportunities that present themselves.

Anticipating the future or reflecting on the past have their benefits, but let's intentionally hold on to the time we have right now and not waste it away.

REFLECTIONS

THINK OF A TIME YOU WERE IN A SITUATION YOU DREADED - PERHAPS A DIFFICULT CLASS OR WHILE WAITING AT THE DMV. WHAT WAS YOUR ATTITUDE GOING INTO THAT SETTING?

A. NERVOUS
B. CONFIDENT

C. FRUSTRATED
D   OTHER_____

WHAT DID YOU DO TO GET THROUGH THAT CIRCUMSTANCE?

A. PRAYED
B. TALKED TO OTHERS

C. TOOK DEEP BREATHS
D   _____

COULD YOU HAVE MANAGED IT BETTER?

A. YES
B. NO

C. MAYBE
D   HMM...

IF YES, WHAT COULD YOU HAVE DONE DIFFERENTLY?

_____
_____
_____

Reframe Game

During professional development sessions with educators, I conduct an activity I call "The Reframe Game." Each participant gets 30 seconds to write about a challenging student and 60 seconds to write about the student's redeeming qualities. The list fills up quickly within the first 30 seconds, but is much more challenging during the next part. The two points to that "game" is first, it's easier to think of the negative, to see faults or things we don't like. Second, there is ALWAYS a flip side. It may take more effort to find it, but good is there.

This summer has been hard with many challenges, but I have tried to reflect on what I can learn from them. It could be patience, letting go, growing in my ability to roll with the punches, or gaining perspective. After a storm caused a power outage in our city, I quickly had to adjust my plans when I realized it would take about a day to restore power. While joking about my situation, someone close to me remarked I couldn't seem to catch a break. At first, I dismissed the comment, but then I realized I had been dealing with a lot of difficulties lately. This realization felt heavy and disheartening, but I reframed my thinking and focused on the positives. I asked myself, "what is the good in this situation?" The good is easy to find if you are looking for it and I noticed that, for me, the outage was temporary. By approaching each problem individually and finding positives in them, I could manage the challenges. If we aren't careful and aware, we can let the weight of hard times take us down.

As educators, you may feel overwhelmed by your responsibilities, such as grading papers, creating lesson plans, attending meetings, and working with students who need individualized education plans. You should acknowledge the challenges but then think about the good. Perhaps you can do that not only professionally but also in your personal lives. Consider playing the reframe game yourself. Instead of seeing everything that is going wrong, maybe try to focus on one thing that is good about the situation. You can acknowledge its difficulties and all you feel about it, but then look for ways to reframe it. This approach can help you cope with difficult situations and make life more enjoyable.

REFLECTIONS

1) Do the activity at the beginning of the blog, or use the "Reframe Game" on a current situation. Is there something in your life that is causing you angst?

_____
_____
_____
_____
_____
_____

2) How can you reframe it? Are there any upsides?

_____
_____
_____
_____
_____
_____

3) What does it look like from a different angle?

_____
_____
_____
_____
_____
_____

4) How does reframing affect your outlook or the way you feel about it?

_____
_____
_____
_____
_____
_____

Pace Yourself

In my opinion, there is no better place than Michigan in the summer. The weather is beautiful, and everyone is outside, enjoying the sunshine. They golf, spend time at one of the many lakes, or tinker in their yard or on a car in the garage. People are out, running, biking, or walking their dogs, kids, or both. I love being outside, especially in the summer.

During the pandemic, walks outside have been a lifesaver for me. On some days, I'm on my own, quietly collecting my thoughts or just zoning out. On others, I've walked with a friend or one of my kids. I also take my headphones and some days I am on a good clip, making my way up and down side streets, while avoiding people. Other days my pace is slower, more of a stroll. I tune into my body and allow it to guide my steps. Regardless of how far or fast I walked, I acknowledge I was taking care of myself that day. It has been a balm for my soul.

During the pandemic, educators were worried, stressed, exasperated, exhausted, and yet determined to do the right thing for their students. Though they made lemonade out of lemons, the pace was unsustainable because of limited resources. In actuality, the pace BEFORE the pandemic was not sustainable.

What is the answer? How can those of us in this arena pace ourselves, no matter the external circumstances? It is hard to pace yourself in this profession, but it is necessary. The first step is to recognize your worth and establish realistic boundaries. Your mental health and wellness are essential to your ability to meet your students' needs. They need you to be at peace, happy and whole.

Think ahead about the coming week or month. Is there a way you can pace yourself? Educators are good at helping students' scaffold and chunk out their work. Can you do that for yourself? Do you need to go SLOW and quiet, or can you juice it up some and push a little harder? Regardless, just know that whatever you have to give is sufficient. Listen to your body; let it inform and guide you. This is your journey; you get to determine your steps. Go at your pace.

REFLECTIONS

Think about your day-to-day activities and check all that apply.

- What I am doing now is sustainable.

- What I am doing now is manageable.

- What I am doing now is not sustainable.

- What I am doing is not manageable.

- Given the power to set my own schedule while maintaining my livelihood, my life would look just as it does now.

- There are things I can do differently to get closer to the lifestyle I desire.

Notes:
_____
_____
_____
_____

Hard But Not Impossible

I've spent the last several weeks conducting professional development sessions with educators and front-line workers on self-care and social, emotional and mental health. Things can feel overwhelming and suffocating for those working in this field. "There is never enough time" is a consistent message I hear. Time to focus on self is easily deferred for later, and prioritizing mental wellness is tough. It is hard, but not impossible.

I'm convinced that opportunities to SLOW down and attend to yourself exist. It may not be an extended vacation to the Bahamas or whatever your idea of a "break" looks like. But during my personal whirlwind of travel, I have been intentional about watching for and capitalizing on any opportunity that presents itself to me to just go SLOW. Sometimes it may just be a couple of minutes before a presentation to sit quietly, connect with myself and breathe; or maybe a meeting ends early, and I can get outside for a quick break and some fresh air. I must be mindful to look for those chances to take a brief self-care moment. I've also learned recently that how I decide to interpret or perceive the moment can make a difference in my self-care. What story am I telling myself about the current situation?

This year I celebrated a milestone birthday and several of my childhood friends are also celebrating with a planned weekend event. Unfortunately, I live two plane rides away from the festivities, so attending would have taken a lot of effort and I'd hardly been home. It weighed heavily on me if I should go or not. In the end, even though I knew I would miss out, I prioritized my wellness. I enjoyed the festivities virtually without adding wear and tear to myself. Like I said, self-care can be hard, but not impossible.

What difficult situations are you facing? As I've spent time with hundreds of professionals over the last several weeks, the stories and experiences recounted to me feel heavy and difficult. Students and those who work with them or on their behalf are struggling. Times are hard, but they are not impossible. Pay attention to ways you can take care of you. They are there if you look for them!

REFLECTIONS

Think about a friend who is going through a hard time and answer the following questions.

What are they experiencing and how can you encourage them ?

_____
_____
_____
_____

1) Do you see any light at the end of the tunnel for them?   Yes   No

2) Is there a way out of their current situation?   Yes   No

Explain_____
_____

3) How can you offer them support?   _____   _____

          _____   _____

Remember that you can transfer these helping and supportive strategies to yourself. Treat yourself the way you would a friend.

S.L.O.W. ROAD RULES

UNDER CONTROL

It's hard when you don't feel in control of a situation. The good news is you have control over the way you respond to it. You can determine how to perceive it and what to do in that moment. Once aware, decide to only manage what you can. Make the most of the moment, even if it's just checking your attitude.

SAVE TIME BY BEING PRESENT

We all face things in life that we don't like. It helps us to appreciate pleasant moments more. It's easy to disengage during tough times and wish our way through them. Sometimes that is a necessary and effective strategy. Other times, we may miss an opportunity to experience something new. Consider attempting to be more present even in the less appealing spaces.

PACE YOURSELF

Part of self-care is listening to ourselves, our body, our emotions, our mind. Pay attention to what you need and in what ways you can afford to expend your energy. Try to check-in with yourself daily at a minimum. Honor yourself.

REFRAME

When you are in the thick of it, it's hard to step back and see things from a different perspective. Sometimes, I find that I just want to be in my feelings about something for a moment. But eventually I want to come out of that fog and keep moving ahead. Reframing helps me get there. Maybe it will help you too.

YOU ARE POSSIBLE

Just like we are eager and willing to help those we care about, we should put that same effort into our own health and wellness. We can find time to care for others, so we can find time to care for ourselves. Follow your own example. Give to yourself as you give to your loved ones. Offer yourself support and encouragement.

ONE SELF-LOVE RULE

Write one of your self-love rules.

_____
_____
_____
_____
_____

QUARTERLY REVIEW

AUG - OCT

BABY STEPS I TOOK

1. _____
2. _____
3. _____

PROUDEST MOMENTS

1. _____
2. _____
3. _____

HIGHLIGHTS

_____
_____
_____

LESSONS I LEARNED

_____
_____
_____

WHAT WORKED

_____
_____
_____
_____
_____
_____
_____

DO BETTER NEXT TIME

_____
_____
_____
_____
_____
_____
_____

IMPROVEMENTS TO MAKE

_____
_____
_____
_____

QUARTERLY PREVIEW

NOV - JAN

THINKING AHEAD

BRIEF MOMENTS AHEAD

1
2
3

I'M EXCITED FOR

I'M CONCERNED ABOUT

MAIN GOALS

MAIN GOALS

IMPORTANT DATES

PART

living
S.L.O.W.™

3

WHIMSICAL WINTER

As the "back to school" season comes to an end, routines are setting in. Ideally, things are humming along. This ushers in the "whimsical winter" season. That's not to say that being whimsical is worry-free, since things can be harried as the winter break approaches. However, times of rest and opportunities to express gratitude imbue a sense of wonder and awe. Hopefully, you can hold on to whimsy while navigating these winter months.

NOVEMBER
- Take a Dare
- Practical Ways to Put Yourself First
- Take Your Time
- Thanks-Getting
- Building Bridges

DECEMBER
- What Comes Around Goes Around
- Practice What You Preach
- Savor the Moment
- You Might as Well
- Ignorance is Bliss

JANUARY
- Feed the Teachers
- Every Day is Like New Year's Day
- First Things First
- New Year, New Me
- Save Yourself

First: Complete the assessment on the following page.

WINTER ASSESSMENT

		YES	NO
1	This time of year, my students, colleagues, and classroom have an established and working routine.	☐	☐
2	I look forward to the upcoming breaks from the very start of this season.	☐	☐
3	I find it easy to incorporate self-care moments during this season since my routines are now in place.	☐	☐
4	The weather has no impact on my mood or behaviors.	☐	☐
5	For this quarter, I have already identified readily available opportunities for self-care.	☐	☐
6	My students' behaviors are more challenging this time of year.	☐	☐
7	I have go-to activities that prepare me to handle situations I may encounter during this time of year.	☐	☐
8	I usually maintain a positive outlook this time of year on work, my students, and my colleagues.	☐	☐

NOTES

NOTES

NOVEMBER

November is usually the time in the year when people focus on gratitude and giving thanks. I'm a big believer that being grateful is an important aspect of self-care. Keeping the things you appreciate at the top of mind; relationships, opportunities to slow down, chances to push yourself to do better, helps boost positivity and self-confidence. All of which can bolster our wellness.

I also don't like to be predictable or go with the expected. I like to add my own twist and creativity to my writings. That is why I deliberately don't talk about "love" explicitly throughout the February posts and why I won't directly encourage you to "give thanks" in these November lessons.

My personal experience suggests that going with the normal anticipated messages can cause some level of disregard, like, "I've heard this before," or "I already know what you are going to say." With these lessons, I don't want you to shut down or tune out automatically. Take time to digest the material and embrace what works for you.

Take a Dare

I'm a competitive person who loves a good dare. A friend challenged me to share on my blog that I got "real" braces. I was anxious about how it would affect my looks, speaking abilities, and self-confidence. Although I'm still self-conscious about them, here I am, taking the dare and being vulnerable.

Though my outward appearance, which also represents self-care, was my initial motivation for getting braces, a couple of orthodontists made it clear it would also benefit my physical health. Knowing that it would help my jaw relax since I'm a "clencher" tipped the scales for me. I felt reassured it could improve my confidence, health, and relaxation, so I was all in!

Now you may ask, what does this have to do with you? Well, you may not need bite alignment or brackets on your teeth, but think about it: What are you in need of? What can help you feel more confident, healthier and/or relaxed? Do you feel vulnerable sharing that need with others?

It's challenging to figure out what you need, let alone share it with someone else, but processing with a friend can help you get to the root of your feelings and needs. Take a quiet moment wherever you are and ask yourself these questions:

- How are you feeling? What helps you let go of the pressures of the day?
- How did the day go or what is your plan for the day ahead?
- What do you need to feel confident as you continue through your day?
- Is there a mantra you can say to yourself?
- What are things you can do to promote a healthier lifestyle?

Taking care of yourself doesn't have to be a long and involved event. Come up with something short and sweet that will help you feel more confident, healthy and/or relaxed. Come on, I dare you!

Reflect on a time when you did something that scared you and you were pushed out of your comfort zone. Then, answer the following questions.

REFLECTIONS

1) What motivated you to push past your fear and attempt the feat anyway?

_____
_____
_____
_____
_____

2) How did you feel afterwards?

_____
_____
_____
_____
_____

3) Any regrets? Would you do it again? Why or why not?

_____
_____
_____
_____
_____

4) What did you learn from that situation?

_____
_____
_____
_____
_____

Practical Ways to Love Yourself First

If you grew up anything like I did, then the idea of loving yourself first was WRONG! I intentionally wrote that in all caps because it wasn't just wrong, it was WRONG! Re-wiring my thinking has been tough. Now, I watch and wait to see what message or lesson the universe sends to teach me. This topic of "loving yourself first" was underscored during an unexpected but invigorating conversation I had with a childhood friend. Reconnecting and sharing our life's paths confirmed how desperately many, particularly women, need to practice loving ourselves first.

Many of us prioritize others' needs above our own, even to the point of sacrificing ourselves. The analogy she used during our conversation was that she is the type of person willing to set herself on fire to keep others warm. Quite a powerful image, isn't it? I experienced this myself, not realizing I had needs and lacking the courage to communicate them. It took years of reassurance to gain the courage to express my needs once I recognized them.

My encouragement to my friend and to all of us is to give yourself permission to love you first and be true to yourself. Start small and use phrases like "not now" or "maybe later" instead of "no" to baby step into this new approach. Ask for time to stop and think before responding to requests. This will benefit not only you but also those around you, as you will have energy and peace of mind to devote to their needs.

Establishing healthy self-care boundaries can be difficult and often requires a change of mindset. Despite the internal self-condemnation, others validate and reassure me when I do set boundaries. Hopefully, I can truly set an example for others to imitate.

Commit to loving yourself first and taking the time to connect with you. Ask yourself what you need today and express those needs to yourself and those who can support you. Remember, you are loved, of course, by others but, most importantly, by you!

REFLECTIONS

Can you think of a time when you put your needs first over other people? What were the circumstances in that situation?

_____
_____
_____
_____
_____
_____
_____

What made you feel safe enough to prioritize your own needs? What gave you the courage to do so? How did that situation play out? How did you feel during and afterwards?

_____
_____
_____
_____
_____
_____
_____
_____
_____
_____
_____

Take Your Time

October was a busy month of travel for me; attending conferences, conducting trainings and networking with old and new contacts. I prepared for the month ahead by planning ways to practice self-care before things kicked in. I also thought through a plan for how to build in self-care during the month. I've written posts before about times when things were busy for me, and I didn't handle it well. I really wanted to try to "do it right" this time. I was curious to see if I could practice what I preach when life was exceptionally frantic.

While supporting teachers and students, in that order, I came home to find we had no hot water! But, easy fix, right? Just relight the pilot light. Not so fast! When that didn't work, I had to call for help while out of town to have the thermocouple replaced, but there was still no hot water.

That left one final option: buy a new water heater and get it installed during the one weekend I'm in town. Fortunately, I found a plumber to do that for me on a Sunday, and hundreds of dollars later, we were back in business. The very next day, as I'm preparing to leave for another trip, I realize our house is freezing. Now, my furnace isn't working. It's at that moment that I stop and decide I have two choices here. I can have another breakdown, which seems reasonable, or I can go S.L.O.W. and take a deep breath and reframe. I determine it is easier and more beneficial to stay calm and keep perspective, asking what is the lesson here?

I thought about all the educators who may feel like "things continue to pile on" for them. Just when they have their curriculum figured out, the district changes it; or they are transferred to a different building. Things can always be worse AND things also get better! I'm grateful that I was determined to take care of myself, and take advantage of slivers of time to go S.L.O.W..

If you are aware, in times of normal chaos or even in unexpected, heightened chaos, you can find time and peace. If you really pay attention, regardless of your circumstances, you can find time for self-care. It's there for the taking.

REFLECTIONS

1) What is your favorite pastime? Why? What do you love about it?

_____
_____
_____
_____
_____

2) If you had a whole day with nothing scheduled, would you do that activity?

_____
_____
_____
_____
_____

3) What would you choose to do with that time?

_____
_____
_____
_____
_____

4) What are ways to embed more enjoyment into your day?

_____
_____
_____
_____
_____

Thanks Getting

It's that time of year when we begin to shift our focus to the upcoming holidays. During the pandemic, we became experts at adjusting and modifying our normal way of life. More time at home to engage with family or friends has been nice. I am not traveling, or shopping or eating out like I used to, which is a cost-savings. Being able to focus on hobbies and health is a blessing as well.

As Thanksgiving approaches, it's a good time to reflect on what we're grateful for. This year, instead of just giving thanks, I suggest we think of ways to get thanks. It may feel weird or selfish, but it is not selfish to focus on our own needs. Look for ways to thank and appreciate yourself. Focus on your strengths and positive attributes and accept your greatness. How can you pat yourself on the back? How can you give yourself gratitude? Think about your positive attributes and accept your greatness.

In a recent dream, I was running around a large house, trying to get to the bathroom just to take a shower. I was being chased by both familiar and unfamiliar people on foot and in a golf cart! I locked them out of open windows and doors while shooing people away. There were groups of people eating and listening to music on the back patio. I woke up taken aback but proud of myself for setting boundaries & staying focused on my needs. I didn't let all the people with their demands stop me from doing what I needed to do. I was kind but assertive when I said, "I can't help you right now. I need a shower."

It doesn't take a dream interpreter to point out the meaning of that dream. How many of us feel we are constantly being pulled on or interrupted by what seems like hundreds of people, when we need the space and time to do the simplest task?

Educators and caregivers often expend considerable energy to support others. That is the nature of our work, giving. This Thanksgiving, why not also get something for yourself? Take time to relax, connect with loved ones, or do something enjoyable. Get those needs met and then give thanks!

REFLECTIONS

Read the below statements and check the ones that apply to you.

- I often pat myself on the back.

- I know my strengths and positive attributes.

- I am good at setting boundaries.

- I often feel I'm being pulled apart or interrupted by others.

Think about things you are grateful for about yourself. What do you appreciate about you? How can you show yourself gratitude? How do you feel when you do that?

_____

_____

_____

_____

_____

_____

_____

_____

Building Bridges

I served as chair for the inaugural Michigan statewide Social Emotional Learning conference, Building Bridges-Breaking Silos. Over 250 people attended virtually and in person. It was a great success, with everyone feeling inspired and loved. It was my first time serving as committee chair and planning the conference was like planning a wedding, with many details to take care of. I was determined to remain focused and stress free throughout the entire experience.

While pulling this conference together, I was also in the throes of a busy "back to school" season with 30 professional development opportunities in an 8-week period. As a self-care promoter, I tried to practice what I preached and show others how to commit to self-care and go S.L.O.W..

I delegated sessions and responsibilities to team members and supported them, trusting them to do their part. As a "control freak" in recovery, I stayed in my lane and avoided micro-managing. I was self-aware and mindful of my warning signs, communicating my needs, and setting boundaries. Overall, I think I did well, and the plan did too.

The more I practice and verbalize my intentions, the easier it gets, and we had a successful event. Before it began, I was sitting with a colleague, reflecting and preparing for a great day ahead. We were at peace and brimming with anticipation of a great day ahead. Despite room for improvement, working collectively helped us share the load.

Ironically, the other takeaway for me from this experience was the importance of building bridges. As educators and caregivers, we all needed each other to collaborate and support, especially as fatigue is high and morale is low. This was especially essential in the climate of COVID fatigue, unmet/unrealistic expectations, and political discord. If we all helped carry the load, it could allow for self-pacing and ultimately self-care.

It was encouraging to see people coming together to support each other and build bridges within the education sector. There was this great energy and passion in the room, and the sessions were beneficial, thought-provoking, and engaging. The real success, though, was us coming together to create new connections, rekindle old ones, and forging new paths. If we commit to building bridges with one another, amazingly, self-care and wellness will become easier.

REFLECTIONS

Remember the "Hands Across America" attempt in the mid-80's? It was a fundraising effort to have people hold hands for 15 minutes across the US.

If you were going to make a human bridge for your community, who would you include and why?

_____
_____
_____
_____

1) I find it easy to build bridges? ● Yes   ● No

2) I am better when I verbalize my intentions.   ● Yes   ● No

Explain_____
_____

3) I can allow others to contribute by: ● _____   ● _____

● _____   ● _____

S.L.O.W. ROAD RULES

I DARE YOU

You may surprise yourself with how strong you can be. Pushing yourself is not necessarily fun or easy, but it's necessary and worth it. Push yourself towards better self-care moments. Set aside your "To-Do" list and embrace your "To-Be" list. Be mindful. Be peaceful. Be intentional. Dare to BE!

TAKE YOUR TIME

It may seem like we are scheduled from start to finish every day. And some days that may be necessary, but hopefully that is the exception and not the rule. Find ways to incorporate fun and delight into your daily activities, even if it's just for a few moments. A little is better than none.

LOVE YOURSELF FIRST

It's difficult to prioritize your own needs. It can feel selfish and maybe others aren't as supportive as you'd like. That doesn't make it less important. Keep practicing. Start small. Build that muscle. Look for opportunities to love yourself, then you will have what you need to love others.

THANKS GETTING

It may be easy to come up with a list of things you're thankful for: family, friends, health, job. But what about things others thank you for: taking a meal to a sick friend, dog sitting for a neighbor? Take a few moments to write yourself a thank you note. Include at least 3 things you are thankful for about yourself!

BUILDING BRIDGES

It is encouraging to know we are not alone in this life. We don't have to shoulder trials on our own. Identify 3 people from your human bridge reflection above. Tell them they are part of your bridge and why. This can help to reinforce those connections.

ONE SELF-LOVE RULE

Write one of your self-love rules.

_____
_____
_____
_____
_____

DECEMBER

You are heading into the last month of the year! If you are anything like me, you come racing into this month on two bald tires, a wing and a prayer, and ready, maybe even desperate, for a break! I have a love-hate relationship with December. I don't appreciate the pressure and heightened expectations society places on us. But I love the awe of the holidays, the sense of togetherness and peace. I also love that the world seems to shut down the last week of the year and provides the opportunity to be still and reflective.

There are times in life when I'm a proponent of tuning out and not being mindful or present. There are occasions when it may be okay to disassociate from what's going on around you. It may be necessary for our mental and emotional survival. Sometimes we can only take in so much mentally before we need to shut down. But as a general rule-of-thumb, research tells us that in most cases, being still and aware is helpful.

I believe December provides us with that space. Review the last year, what are your moments of glows? What are your moments of growth? How have you evolved and how can you improve? Perhaps you like to make resolutions. What are your dreams, ambitions, goals, and plans? I look forward to new chapters. I hope in this final chapter, these lessons help you get excited about your future and the chances you have to take care of you. You are a gift!

What Comes Around Goes Around

I believe in the law of attraction, and I also believe that what you put into the world is what you get out of it. I pride myself on being tuned into other people and what they are feeling. I think this emotional intelligence was something that I inherited from my parents, both of whom were educators and have a special way of empathizing with other people. I learned early on to "put myself in someone else's shoes." I attribute this upbringing to my choice to pursue a career in social work.

Sometimes, being so aware of other's needs, I can neglect my own. It's important to find the balance, to attend to others and yet still prioritize your own self-care.

There is so much negativity and hatred in our world today, so I can feel overpowered and paralyzed by all I think needs to be improved, changed, and fixed. What can one little social worker like me do? I can love. And you can too. Recently, my neighbor pulled in from work and shared with me about her bad day, so I sent over a small bottle of wine and a note of encouragement. That same week, a parent I know through my daughter's team lost a family member. I took a few minutes to make some banana bread and sent it, along with a note, to their family.

So why are these two examples significant? Well, this past month has been very challenging for my family. Our beloved pet passed away and a week later, my daughter had a serious health issue that landed her in the ER along with a plethora of follow-up visits. It was a physically and emotionally taxing week. However, friends, neighbors, and family members sent gifts, cards and messages that made a tremendous difference in our time of need. So it felt natural to want to give back.

What does this mean for you? Perhaps you should take advantage of the opportunities to show love to others around you. A simple smile and hello can help someone through a tough time. And just when you need it, kindness will come knocking at your door.

REFLECTIONS

1) When was the last time you encouraged someone in need?

2) Recall and write down a time when you were in need.

3) How did others encourage you?

4) How did it lift your spirits?

Practice What You Preach

Perhaps you have heard the adage, "you teach what you need to learn." Well, the last six weeks, I've been thrilled to share my passion with so many people around the state and country.

Nevertheless, being on the road so much recently, I noticed my level of tolerance waning. Usually a gracious driver, I've been teeter tottering near the "road rage" line. In addition, I've seen a different side of myself after conferences. The more miles I traveled, the more intolerant I became.

Racing back from my last overnight trip of the season, I realized the negative energy I had been releasing was not attractive. I strive to be an example for people to take care of themselves and support those around them, yet I was compounding negativity. The irony of my work - to create positive environments for learning - set in; none of that involves losing it with people. It was humbling to realize that I hadn't been following my advice of taking time for myself by prioritizing my needs and establishing boundaries.

Now, here we find ourselves, knee-deep in the holiday season that should fill us with gratitude and reflection rather than create a sense of frenzy. However, I refuse to give in to the holiday hoopla.

This time of year, I want to remind you to practice patience, slow down and focus on the things you value. Show love to yourself and others and make memories with family and friends. I will intentionally continue to practice the things I preach and hope you will do the same. We will all be better off and have a merrier holiday.

REFLECTIONS

WHAT ARE YOUR OWN PERSONAL WARNING SIGNS THAT DENOTE WHEN YOU ARE RUNNING LOW ON ENERGY AND NEED A SELF-CARE BREAK?

A. IRRITABLE

B. IMPATIENT

C. OTHER_____

D. CRITICAL

E. TEARY-EYED

F. OTHER_____

HOW DO YOU RESPOND WHEN YOU SEE THOSE ALERTS?

_____

_____

_____

HOW OFTEN DO THESE BEHAVIORS SHOW THEMSELVES?

A. DAILY

B. PERIODICALLY

C. FREQUENTLY

D RARELY

WHAT CAN YOU DO TO PREVENT THESE REACTIONS?

A. _____

B. _____

C. _____

D _____

Savor the Moment

Most of us have just enjoyed time with family and friends, gathered to give thanks and hopefully partook of a savory meal. Can you remember the smell of the turkey or ham cooking? Or the taste of dessert, that you were too full to eat but did, anyway? The sights of décor and sounds of people laughing and kids playing, if done right, can be a wonderful experience, especially if we savor the moment. Appreciate the company, relish the food prepared, embrace the time to relax and refresh. Take it all in. SLOWLY.

This year more than previous years, I couldn't wait to get to Thanksgiving. I was committed to and intentional about practicing what I preach. I paid attention and embedded some self-care as I traversed North America, training others on self-care. I used my voice to say "No" to things that I thought would sap energy that I needed to reserve for later situations. I established boundaries and spoke my truth, all things I encourage others to do.

I also got better at delegating, letting other people handle things I didn't need to be involved in. Not only does this approach save me time and energy, but it allows other people to learn, grow and take care of their own business.

Over the past 6 weeks, I was able to savor many moments - on planes, in cabs, or silent time in my hotel rooms. I've tried to take advantage of these moments by closing my eyes, taking breaths, and being mindful of the sights and sounds around me. We all have opportunities to be in the present and savor the moment, if we simply take the time to notice.

As you enter the busy holiday season, and reflect on the past year, take time to be with your loved ones and also find time to be alone. It is easy to get caught up in the holiday season flurry, scheduling time to be with family and friends, traveling, holiday parties, shopping, cooking and gift exchanging. It can be over and done before we know it. Focus on what you need and take the time to rejuvenate for the new year. Savor the moments. You deserve it!

REFLECTIONS

Consider a time you were able to enjoy a special meal. What made it so special? How was the food? Who was with you? Why?

_____
_____
_____
_____
_____
_____
_____

What are moments you can savor during your work day? Are their times with coworkers or students that stand out to you?

_____
_____
_____
_____
_____
_____
_____
_____
_____
_____
_____

The Gift That Keeps on Giving

We're finally heading into the end of the year and launching into the gift-giving season. If you are anything like me, you enjoy giving gifts to others. Some of my favorite people have birthdays right around the holidays. I think about each person's interests or what's going on in their life. I'm intentional as I contemplate what they would want. My favorite part is when I offer it to them, and watch their reaction, especially if I got it "right." That brings me so much joy, it fills me up too.

I have another friend who loves to cook and bake. Each year as her children were growing up, for their birthdays she would make them a cake from scratch. She shared she wouldn't let anyone else in the kitchen so she could intentionally think about the person for whom she was baking adding in love as an important ingredient.

My lessons are often about being intentional. I highlight the need to SLOW down, to be self-aware, and in tune with your own needs. Instead of operating on autopilot, I encourage you to take (or make) time to think about yourself for a change. What do you need right now at this moment?

In my family, we have an inside joke. Sometimes we may purchase a gift for ourselves during the holidays, something we see on sale that we think is too good of a deal to pass up. We will wrap it and put it under the tree with a label, "To: Me From: Me." Those are gifts that are guaranteed to please, the ones you pick out for yourself.

Perhaps you should try that this year. Is there something you really want? Maybe it's something you purchase, a massage, a book, a hotel room. My best friend said to tell you, "Don't feel guilty about spending money and investing in yourself. You work hard and deserve it!" It could also be something that doesn't carry a price tag but can be invaluable to your own self-care. Allowing you to refuel so you can be happy, healthy, and whole to meet the needs of those around you. Those are my favorite gifts, the ones that keep on giving! Happy Holidays!

REFLECTIONS

Write about your favorite gift as a child and/or as an adult. Why did you want it?

Notes:
_____
_____
_____
_____

Why was it your favorite? How did you feel receiving it/them?

Notes:
_____
_____
_____
_____

What's a gift you can give yourself right now?

Notes:
_____
_____
_____
_____

Back to Basics

As I type this, I'm sitting on a plane. I'll be gone for three days. Typically, I over pack, but a friend challenged me to attempt to pack light and carry on my luggage instead of my typical check-it. So, I took the challenge and only brought the basics.

Educators are struggling this year more than ever citing staff shortage, exhaustion, the pressure to make up for learning loss, and addressing social-emotional needs. They are trying to carry on as normal as possible, but it's impossible. There's a way to relieve the pressure educators are under, but it's bigger than me; it's systemic. My commitment and message about educator self-care won't change the system, but I'm determined to help in my small way.

I read a blog post from Sean Slade that discussed the importance of self-care for teachers. They used the metaphor of a burning building, with teachers being pulled out of the fire and then put back in. I shared this analogy in several meetings and professional development sessions to emphasize the challenge of wanting to support teachers while self-care isn't enough. I likened it to giving teachers ice packs and sending them back into the burning building.

Even though I know it isn't enough, I am still convinced it's necessary. Self-care is an act of survival. It may not fix everything, but we must fight for our own well-being, even amid chaos. So, how do we do that? I believe we get back to the following basics:

- Have the courage to say no. You don't have to be everything to everyone.
- Trim down the to do list. What can wait? What MUST be done?
- Find something for which to be grateful. Hold on to that.
- Live in the land of good enough. Things don't have to be perfect.
- Remember, you are not alone. Tag team, divide and conquer, ask for help.

I hope you can reflect on these things and travel as light as possible on this part of your journey. I'll help you put things in the overhead compartment. Sending you love and light!

REFLECTIONS

Think about your work as an educator or service professional.

What are some of your greatest challenges?

_____
_____
_____
_____

1) Which of these are the most challenging for you?

　Saying no　　　　Being thankful

　Trim down　　　　Getting help

2. Think about just the basics. What are ways you can lighten your load?

_____
_____
_____
_____
_____
_____
_____

3. Write down one way you will commit to just the basics.

_____
_____
_____
_____
_____
_____
_____

S.L.O.W. ROAD RULES

GIVE AND TAKE

It's difficult to let others do for us, especially when we are used to doing for others so often. Allowing others to give to you not only helps you, but it helps them too. The give and take reciprocity puts positive energy into the universe. It feels good to give and subsequently it is good to take too. Make the most of BOTH opportunities as they arise.

PRACTICE WHAT YOU PREACH

It takes self-awareness, humility, and practice to notice your own warning signs. They start off subtly and get louder if you ignore them. You can't deny your emotions forever. Pay attention to them. Ask others who know you well and feel safe to help you spot them if you need help. It's for the best!

SAVOR THE MOMENT

Use the exercise about food to consider ways you can be more mindful throughout your day - not just when you eat, but also when there are moments you can tap into for self-care. Try to savor those opportunities, even if they are brief. They can add up to make a difference. Soak them up!

THE GIFT THAT KEEPS ON GIVING

Remember, you are a gift! Look forward to time with yourself with gratitude and excitement. Let the gift of you become your focus for a set amount of time. Enjoy the time you have with THE one, you!

BACK TO BASICS

It takes being thoughtful to consider sticking to the basics. Adding on more just happens by default if we aren't careful. Look ahead, think about ways to trim the fat, avoid any extras, and try to keep things as simple as possible. This can be freeing and allows for more space to breathe.

ONE SELF-LOVE RULE

Write one of your self-love rules.

_____
_____
_____
_____

JANUARY

Being raised by two Type A personalities influenced my love for checklists, plans, and rules. As a child, I created long lists of New Year's Resolutions:

- Share my toys (or clothes as I got older).
- Be nice to my sisters.
- Be less selfish.
- Eat less junk food.

Those were consistently on my list, and I attempted to maintain them, for the most part, as best as I could. As I matured, my list evolved.

- Workout more.
- Eat healthier.
- Be nice to my husband.

Like most people, I started off strong with those well-intentioned commitments, but I scarcely followed through. The less I committed to them, the more jaded I became. Resolutions eventually became an act of futility. "Why bother?" I wasn't going to follow through anyway.

In recent years, I've found myself with a renewed spirit of resolutions, maintaining a more realistic expectation of one significant resolution a year. I've also decided to pair one word that signifies the theme of the year. They've provided a foundation for the perspective with which I'm entering the new year: mindful, peaceful, and inspirational. How you infuse the spirit of the new year is entirely up to you, but I offer the perspectives provided in the January lessons to rouse a desire to prioritize yourself and your well-being.

Feed the Teachers, So They Don't Eat the Kids

Education is at the core of who I am. My father was a special education teacher, and my mother was a school counselor. I married a high school teacher. In the last decade, I've been a school social worker and have done a fair share of federal grant-funded contracted work with the state Department of Education. I've worked with so many schools and districts that I can hardly remember them all. I've seen education from many angles and many the perspectives.

Over my tenure in education, especially with schools deemed "underperforming," my primary focus has been on meeting the multifaceted mental health needs of students: Improving school climate and culture, providing access to mental health services, adopting policies and procedures to support all students, and training school personnel. All of these components are crucial to the academic success of students.

However, I realize–along with many other professionals in this field–that if we don't also prioritize the well-being of the adults in the building, it impedes our efforts to help the youth. It's illogical to expect adults who are beat down, unsupported, exhausted, undervalued, and overworked to educate our next generation effectively, especially when many of them exhibit the same conditions. We must fill up (feed) our educators. Help them be whole so they can support and nourish our youth, fill them up and help them, too, to be whole.

Though my intention is to provide ideas and suggestions to "Feed the Teachers," this doesn't exclude administrators, other adult faculty in a school building, or any other profession. We could all benefit from some self-care.

This process offers some quick or easy fixes, things that take a few minutes at most and can carry you throughout the day. Ultimately, in this fast-paced world, I hope we can learn to go S.L.O.W..

REFLECTIONS

WHAT ARE THINGS IN YOUR LIFE THAT FEED YOU, YOUR SOUL, YOUR ENERGY?

A. SERVICE TO OTHERS   C. TIME WITH FAMILY
B. ALONE TIME   D   OTHER_____

WHAT THINGS PREVENT YOU FROM "FEEDING" YOUR SPIRIT?

A. _____   C. _____
B. _____   D   _____

WHAT ACTIVITIES CAN YOU PRIORITIZE FOR YOURSELF THIS WEEK?

A. EXERCISE   C. FUN DAY TRIP
B. MEDITATION   D   OTHER_____

WHO ARE THE PEOPLE YOU CAN COUNT ON TO SUPPORT YOUR BRIEF SELF-CARE MOMENTS AND HAVE A HEALTHY IMPACT ON YOUR DAY?

A. _____   C. _____
B. _____   D   _____

Every Day is Like New Year's Day

The new year is a time of great anticipation and excitement. It's the perfect opportunity to start anew and set resolutions to motivate and measure personal growth.

For years, I would make a laundry list of goals for the months ahead but lacked staying power with my resolutions. I found it hard to change ingrained habits so that lead to discouragement and apathy and ultimately resulted in me losing or forgetting my list. So, a few years ago I gave up on making New Year's resolutions and now work on overall goals to become a better version of myself. Some goals are long-term, five or more years, while others are annual or even daily. Here, we'll focus on the short-term goals.

Long-term goals and ambitions are important, but it is the daily, bite-sized actions that make a difference. Since "S.L.O.W. and steady wins the race," these incremental changes, though seemingly insignificant, can build on each other to make a big impact. Whether it's getting eight hours of sleep or working out every day, these lofty but unrealistic goals can feel very daunting. Rather, add a little time to one night's rest or try taking the stairs at work. These changes can get you moving, don't take much time, and can help towards healthy practices.

Perhaps your goal isn't one of those two "stereotypical" areas. It could be to stay positive in your high stress career or learn to navigate life's choppy waters with a bit more self-preservation. Showing gratitude is one of my favorite practices. Reflecting on things I'm grateful for helps me reframe my day and maintain a solution-oriented mindset. With this daily goal approach, you get to reframe and celebrate more frequently. You set out to make your small daily change and when it happens, you can pat yourself on the back. Who doesn't want that every day?

But what about those days that don't go as well, and you can't take your victory lap? Well, there's good news there too. This tactic makes it feel like every day is New Year's day. You get a fresh start with each new day, just like each new year. Life renews itself every day. Isn't that refreshing? Have a Happy New Year–daily!

REFLECTIONS

Read the below statements and check the ones that apply to you.

○ I have things I can find to celebrate each day.

○ I set goals but find it hard to have "staying power."

○ I have no problem achieving any goal I set for myself.

○ I can find things to be grateful for each day.

○ I hate setting goals, even short term ones.

○ I enjoy setting both short and long term goals.

Notes:

_____

_____

_____

_____

First Things First

Some years are harder than others, filled with tough decisions and experiences. In 2018, I was in a "funk" for weeks, if not months. As I welcomed the holiday break, my sister and I talked about how that school year felt more tense than years before. Educators and colleagues I worked with were unusually exhausted.

However, as we all know, good can come from enduring challenging times. We learn perseverance, valuable lessons, and grow in our tenacity. As obvious as this may sound, I'm glad a new year starts after an old year ends. We can take what we learn from the old year and enter a new year with new resolve.

During the holidays, after all the hustle and bustle has died down, people prioritize family and relaxation. We disengage from the world, spend quality time with loved ones and rest, connect, laugh, eat, sleep, give, and get. This is a perfect way to end the year and begin a new one, refreshed and ready to forge ahead. A new year is like a clean slate. You get to write this chapter in your life's story. I hope that as you scribe your future, this new year, you put first things first.

What are the values that matter most? For me, family, hard work, legacy, laughter, sleep, love, friendships, quiet-time, health, and well-being are important. If you hold on to these values, try to avoid autopilot and prioritize the things that matter, including yourself, to maintain your rest and relaxation.

Our work as educators is vital to shaping young lives. To have the greatest influence, we must prioritize our own health—mentally, emotionally, and physically. Self-care may seem unattainable and too time intensive, however, I know that even small steps toward taking care of you can make a big difference.

On your way to work, try listening to relaxing music or nothing at all and take a few moments to express your gratitude. Going S.L.O.W. and appreciating the little things in life can help to replenish your spirit. Reach out to those around you and let them know how much you appreciate them. Start this New Year by putting first things first and enjoying the many benefits it brings. Happy New Year!

REFLECTIONS

1) What/Who are your priorities in life?

_____
_____
_____
_____
_____
_____

2) What are things/people you value the most?

_____
_____
_____
_____
_____
_____

3) Think about how you demonstrate the significance of those things/people. Now consider how you can show that same level of value and importance to yourself.

_____
_____
_____
_____
_____
_____

4) What is a need you have? What is one way you can put that need first?

_____
_____
_____
_____
_____
_____

New Year, New Me

I recently launched AchievHER ™, a spinoff of Living S.L.O.W., which focuses on empowering women through self-care, inspiration, and empowerment. It has been a great learning experience. With plenty of other responsibilities such as running a business, raising a family, and supporting a parent, I had plenty of opportunity to practice self-care. I also understand I need to do the very things I'm encouraging others to do.

My first AchievHER launch was successful, with many pre-orders for two colorful quotes and, not surprisingly, "New Year New Me" was the top choice. However, the material ordered from the manufacturer was unusable. I could have panicked and forged ahead, but I remembered to SLOW down. I made the courageous choice to send them back and work with someone else.

Of course, that prompted a mad dash, and I ultimately made a poor business decision and opted for a mediocre alternative. I felt uneasy and tried to justify my decision, but I had settled against my vision. Maybe you have felt that too, the queasy feeling when you go against your gut or values. I was tempted to ignore my feelings but regrouped instead and figured out a plan of action. I could then get a good night's sleep and the next day take responsibility for all my new customers and set things right.

One thing I noticed through all the flurry of launching this new arm of Living S.L.O.W. is that if I'm not careful, I can lose my voice and forget who I am and what I need. I imagine this can happen to others, like educators who kick into default mode as the break draws closer. The days before a holiday break are a perfect storm, time winding down and pressure increasing, while energy wains. We forget about ourselves and neglect our values instead of being true to ourselves.

So, as the New Year begins, be determined to go S.L.O.W., staying committed to your values and using your voice. Regardless of what the new year holds, be strong, empowered, healthy and full of self-love. It's a New Year, be a New You!

REFLECTIONS

Think for a moment about who you are, not just what you do or the roles you play in life but what makes you you.

What are the attributes my friends attribute to me?

_____

_____

_____

_____

1) It is hard to think of my unique attributes.	○ Yes		○ No

2) Four of my unique attributes are:	○ _____		○ _____
	○ _____		○ _____

3) Every year, I look forward to a "New Year, New Me."	○ Yes		○ No

Save Yourself

We did it! We made it to a new year! As the years go by and people reflect on "lessons learned" from 2020, there are recurring themes: realization that we can get by with less, the joy of spending more time at home and with family, a greater appreciation for educators and health care staff and other essential workers, and a recognition that our "normal" life was good and yet could be improved. It's a great way to start a new year!

I took the idea of "self-preservation" into the new year, which ironically came up later in two different conversations. I just chuckled to myself and said, "Ok, universe, I get it. Self-preservation it is."

January is the birth month of my firstborn, now in his mid-twenties, who was born prematurely at 3.2 lbs. He spent 5 weeks in the NICU before coming home. We were thrilled yet terrified as first-time parents since he was a mere four pounds. Everything about him was fragile, so we had to be very cognizant of keeping him healthy by sterilizing everything and restricting visitors with any signs of illness. We were on vigilant "son-preservation" duty.

We go to extraordinary lengths to protect our physical health. Why not our emotional health? Why can't we make that same commitment to preserve our own emotional and mental well-being? I have inserted self-preservation practices into my daily routine. It takes some forethought and sometimes a little maneuvering, but it pays off in the end. Save time in your schedule for you, even if for just a few minutes. Think about what you need?

As professionals who work in education, or any field for that matter, now more than ever, it's vital that you prioritize your own self-care. It doesn't have to take a lot, small acts of kindness you would naturally give to others, also turn, and give to yourself! We need you; you need you. Save your time, save your energy, save your well-being, save yourself! Happy New Year!

REFLECTIONS

How is your emotional health? On a scale from 1 to 10, rate how you are feeling emotionally (10 being "I'm on top of the world"). Why did you select that rating?

_____
_____
_____
_____
_____
_____
_____
_____

What are the things that you considered as you selected your number? What can you do to improve that number, if needed?

_____
_____
_____
_____
_____
_____
_____
_____
_____
_____
_____

S.L.O.W. ROAD RULES

FEED THE TEACHERS

Make a commitment to prioritize things in your life as part of your self-care. Identify one thing you can do for yourself today to help fill your cup. Then pick something for the next day. These should be small, simple things. Don't worry about the big picture–rather, just make a small commitment every day. Do it for a few days and see how it feels.

EVERY DAY IS NEW YEAR'S DAY

Notice your growth and progress in a particular area of your life. Hold on to that victory as you move forward each week. Share it with a safe person in your life so they can celebrate with you. Remember each win, even small ones, when things get hard. Let that bolster you. And if you have a hard time remembering, your friend can remind you too.

FIRST THINGS FIRST

It isn't always easy and takes practice to even recognize your own needs, let alone to prioritize them. Take some time to write about some of your needs. Then identify which one you will focus on first. You can do it! I believe in you!

NEW YEAR, NEW ME

Read over your unique traits. Consider writing them on notecards and putting them in places you can easily see. Let them serve as reminders of your value as you navigate through your day. Seeing your value can help motivate you to take care of yourself. You deserve it!

SAVE YOURSELF

Share your self-preservation number with a close confidant. Maybe they can share theirs with you as well. Commit to supporting one another as you improve your rating. Remember, our emotional well-being is just as important as our physical health.

ONE SELF-LOVE RULE

Write one of your self-love rules.

_____

_____

_____

_____

_____

QUARTERLY REVIEW

NOV - JAN

BABY STEPS I TOOK

1 _____
2 _____
3 _____

PROUDEST MOMENTS

1 _____
2 _____
3 _____

HIGHLIGHTS

_____
_____
_____

LESSONS I LEARNED

_____
_____
_____

WHAT WORKED

_____
_____
_____
_____
_____
_____

DO BETTER NEXT TIME

_____
_____
_____
_____
_____
_____

IMPROVEMENTS TO MAKE

_____
_____
_____
_____

QUARTERLY PREVIEW

FEB - APR

THINKING AHEAD

BRIEF MOMENTS AHEAD

1
2
3

I'M EXCITED FOR

I'M CONCERNED ABOUT

MAIN GOALS

MAIN GOALS

IMPORTANT DATES

PART

living
S.L.O.W.™

4

SPRING TOWARD THE FINISH LINE

This season of the school year brings various experiences. Classes have jelled and there's a level of normalcy and expectations have been established. However, there can be added pressure to meet all academic benchmarks as for educator's this is also a season of "testing." It's important to maintain your commitment to your own wellness while propelling yourself and your students ahead through the spring season.

FEBRUARY
- Living S.L.O.W.
- Mind Over Matter
- Faith Over Fear
- Running Fast
- Shouldn't Have to Be Like This

MARCH
- 5 Easy Tips for Living S.L.O.W.
- Prioritizing You Doesn't Bode Well for Me
- Take Back Your Power
- Charged Up
- Good for You

APRIL
- Honesty is the Best Policy
- Stay in Your Lane
- One Step at a Time
- Silver Linings
- You Are Not Alone

First: Complete the assessment on the following page.

SPRING ASSESSMENT

		YES	NO
1	I have set reasonable boundaries for myself both in and out of the classroom.	☐	☐
2	I am prepared to identify and hold on to great moments throughout my day.	☐	☐
3	I have plans in place to help my students and me enjoy school in the spring.	☐	☐
4	I have mood enhancing activities that can add a spring in my step this quarter?	☐	☐
5	For this quarter, I am prepared to see the best in my students.	☐	☐
6	I am mentally, physically, and emotionally prepared to support my colleagues.	☐	☐
7	I am ready, willing, and able to help my students fully learn the material.	☐	☐
8	I have more than one activity ready to improve student learning and maintain my sanity.	☐	☐

NOTES

NOTES

FEBRUARY

The month of February is one of my favorites, for a couple of reasons. I love that it is a short month during winter-my least favorite season because it moves us to spring more quickly. And of course, there is a deliberate focus on love and what's not to like about love?

February is a natural time to pay extra attention to those you care about. We set aside special date time and purchase gifts to celebrate relationships, romance, and connection.

February is also an opportunity to intentionally practice some self-love. I've heard it said, "You can't truly accept love from others until you can accept it from yourself." Learning to love yourself can be difficult. I get groans and moans sometimes in my workshops when we do activities around ways to love yourself. Set aside some special date time for yourself! How can you celebrate connecting with yourself? What are things you love about yourself? Remember that loving yourself first can give you the energy needed to fully love others. Enjoy these lessons from the month of love!

Living S.L.O.W.

Life has a tendency to put us in the fast lane. Many times I find myself singing, "Life in the fast lane..." by the Eagles, while I'm running from place to place. I developed the acronym S.L.O.W.© to help me keep perspective in crazy times. I hope you use the suggestions in this book to help you slow down. Here goes!

S-*Stick to your values*
Sometimes we can feel stress when faced with various decisions. There can be tough choices to be made at work, or with family or friends, in our communities or even within ourselves. It helps me to stop, slow down and think about "what do I value?", "what is important to me?" Letting what you truly believe and stand for guide you in your decision making allows you to be true to yourself, and at peace.

L-*Love yourself then others*
My parents taught me as a child that I should love others over myself and to put others first. There is good in that, to be mindful of other people and their needs. But as I matured, I've learned that if I am empty, my energy is spent, and I'm running on fumes, I'm no good for anyone! Learn to make yourself a priority.

O-*Only apologize Once*
This is true for everyone, but especially women who are typically socialized to apologize for everything. We walk past someone in a grocery store aisle and say, "sorry" if we get too close. Why do we do that? Whether you're on autopilot or insecure, say it once, mean it, and move on.

W-*Wait and Watch*
This piece of the acronym is one of the most difficult and my favorite. When circumstances become challenging, I have to consciously step away. It helps to insert space and time to wait and watch. I encourage you to do the same. It saves a lot of energy and stress.

I hope this acronym offers some food for thought and a way to reframe how we function in our lives in the fast lane.

REFLECTIONS

1) Review the 4 tenets of Living S.L.O.W. acronym. Which one resonates with you the most?

_____
_____
_____
_____
_____

2) What is the easiest for you to hold to? Why?

_____
_____
_____
_____
_____

3) Which is the most difficult? Why?

_____
_____
_____
_____
_____

4) What is one way you can go to the next step in your S.L.O.W. endeavor?

_____
_____
_____
_____

Mind Over Matter

One holiday season, my family was fortunate enough to take a trip to Mexico for just over a week. We had adopted my daughter, who is of Mexican descent, so we thought it was a great opportunity to learn about her culture. It was an amazing trip despite us all having head colds almost the whole time. I realized as I was sitting at the base of the ruins in Coba, the day I felt the worst, how exceptional it is that as people we can rally when we really need to. It's impressive the power our mind and willpower have over us physically. We see it all the time with athletes. They push through their physical pain to finish the race or score the goal or win the game.

This "mind over matter" ability can help us mentally/emotionally in tough decisions, uncomfortable conversations, obligations, or even simple tasks.
I had a meeting I was dreading, and I was looking for a way to get out of going. On my drive there, I reframed my thoughts and feelings and thought of positive outcomes. Surprisingly, it ended up being the best meeting I'd had with this group of educators and was a real turning point for them.

Are there times throughout your week where you could use a little mind over matter technique? What about when you've been asked the same question about an assignment for the 100th time by the 100th student? Or before heading into a staff meeting or professional development session when you'd much rather be grading papers? Or what about when that alarm goes off in the morning to signal it's time for your workout, or the day, to begin?

Life gives us plenty of opportunities to practice changing our perspective and focus on the good in sometimes undesirable situations, which can often make them more desirable. Try using "mind over matter" yourself this week and see how it goes. I hope you experience more positivity than you think you will.

REFLECTIONS

THINK ABOUT A TIME WHEN YOU USED THE STRATEGY "MIND OVER MATTER." WHAT HAPPENED?

_____
_____
_____
_____

WHAT INSPIRED YOU TO USE THAT APPROACH?

_____
_____
_____
_____

WHAT BENEFITS DID YOU NOTICE FROM EMPLOYING "MIND OVER MATTER?"

_____
_____
_____
_____

LIST 4 PEOPLE WHO HAVE SHOWN YOU GREAT EXAMPLES OF SUCCESSFULLY USING "MIND OVER MATTER."

_____
_____
_____
_____

Faith Over Fear

It was the day after Super Bowl Sunday, 1998. I was pregnant with my firstborn and was so sick that I ended up in the ER completely dehydrated. Upon admittance, they immediately prepped me for emergency surgery. I was going to give birth to my son that day, exactly two months to the day before his actual due date. In fact, it was so urgent that the physician couldn't wait for the epidural anesthesia to take effect before making her incision into my abdomen. It was excruciatingly painful until the medicine kicked in.

My son weighed a whopping three pounds and spent five weeks in the NICU, developing his lung capacity, ability to eat and to gain weight. Though I was mostly out of it, those in my orbit remind me of the fear of that day. There were so many unknowns. Yet there really wasn't anything we could do but watch and wait.

As I've shared in a previous lesson, I've had difficult years with plenty of opportunities to be fearful. I had to face those fears with faith, believe good would come even from difficulty, and remember times when that's proven to be true already.

Maybe you are going through a time right now that feels uncertain. It can be tempting to take matters into your own hands and manipulate the outcome. But I'm learning that often times, things work out the way they were intended. This helps my fears subside and I hope it does the same for you.

Experiment the next time things seem to be coming apart at the seams. Perhaps you have a difficult deadline or personal crisis looming. See what happens if you take a breath and let it all unfold in time. I suspect you will feel more at peace, knowing that it can all work out in the end just the way it should.

I am grateful for that life-threatening event over two decades ago and even for all the hard times since then. They have served a purpose and I'm stronger today because of them. I hope that is the case for you as well. Facing your fears with faith, believing in a better tomorrow, allows you to be your best in the end.

REFLECTIONS

Reflect on a time when you were in a situation that caused you to feel afraid. How did you respond? Did you try to take control?

_____
_____
_____
_____
_____
_____
_____
_____

What was your energy level? How did things unfold?

_____
_____
_____
_____
_____
_____
_____
_____
_____
_____
_____
_____

Running Fast

Is it just me or does it feel like we hit the ground running after the holidays? Typically, it feels like we ramp back into "reality" progressively. I have also noticed the last few years how hard it is for me to unplug, whether I'm going on vacation or just getting some time off work, but once I do, it's becoming increasingly harder to plug back in.

Someone said it's because of my age, which could be a viable explanation. I especially noticed that process this year. I was enjoying my quieter days, slower pace, and felt resistance to jumping back into the rat race. It made me wonder, like I have at other times, do we really have to move as fast as we are? We are living in a world of instant gratification. I think everyone senses it, adults and students alike. It's hard to wait, be patient, go slow.

I am convinced it does not have to be like this, at least not all the time. And I am pretty certain I am not the only one feeling this way. Not only have I recognized it in my own life, but because of my renewed awareness, I see it in others around me as well.

Can you think of times when this has happened to you? Perhaps an administrator's poor decision caused repercussions that trickled down to you and your colleagues. Or perhaps your quick reaction to a student discourages them and they don't perform as well academically. It can set off a chain reaction.

I believe the same can happen if we don't pace ourselves intentionally. It could be as simple as taking a few breaths before responding to a student, an email, a parent, or a colleague. Maybe you ask someone to give you some time to think through a situation which helps them to rethink as well.

Another approach to help you go S.L.O.W. could include setting a deadline that feels more reasonable for you. You may not always have the luxury to incorporate these strategies, but I believe we have opportunities to use them that we may be missing. Commit to the Living S.L.O.W. mission, so you don't have to run so fast.

REFLECTIONS

Read the below statements and check the ones that apply to you.

○ I am usually in a rush to get things done.

○ I feel like my schedule runs my life.

○ I enjoy keeping a fast pace when I do things.

○ Keeping a fast pace is exhausting for me.

○ I need to implement S.L.O.W. down strategies.

○ I know of 3 areas in my life where I can intentionally slow down. Write them below.

Notes:

_____

_____

_____

_____

Shouldn't Have to Be Like This

At a two-day Teacher Self-Care virtual conference with hundreds of educators from around the world, various presenters shared openly and honestly from their lives, offering their classroom experience over many years. It was inspiring to hear their stories of how they've overcome. However, throughout the presentations, I was acutely aware that, as several speakers shared their stories, there was a recurring theme. These few educators had to go through extremely challenging health complications before they began to really focus on their own self-care. Two of them mentioned being required to take doctor ordered medical leaves. A couple of others talked about having no other choice but to leave the profession they LOVED to protect their health and well-being.

As the conference concluded, I logged off feeling many emotions. Besides feeling inspired and impressed by the focus on self-care, I was further motivated to continue my endeavor to support educators and their well-being. Classrooms and schools shouldn't be war zones. They should be safe havens, places of support, inclusion, and positivity.

We have to realize our worth, not just what we contribute to a classroom or work setting, but who we are as people. Remember who you are and what you stand for. Hold on to those values. Be empowered to protect and provide for yourself. Then identify who in your life are the truth tellers, but also your cheerleaders? These are the people that not only have your back, but they have your heart. They can be honest with you while also encouraging you simultaneously.

We all need people who can offer us both things, opportunities to better ourselves, along with the recognition of the good we bring to the world. I'm not sure if the conference presenters had people in their lives asking them to step back, to take care of themselves, and they just didn't heed the warnings. But what I am sure about is I ask that of you and me. Let's remember our value and take care of ourselves.

REFLECTIONS

Do a body scan.

How are you feeling physically? ?

_____
_____
_____
_____

1) I carry my tension internally?   ○ Yes   ○ No

2) I feel stress in my...   ○ Neck   ○ Back

          ○ Shoulders   ○ All of the above

3) I have things I can do to alleviate stress and tension. If yes, write them here.   ○ Yes   ○ No

- -
- -
- -

S.L.O.W. ROAD RULES

LIVING S.L.O.W.

Consider how you will adopt a S.L.O.W. mindset in your daily life. Write down one thing you will do differently as you move forward.

MIND OVER MATTER

Look for other opportunities to practice this strategy. Notice how it potentially changes your mood, attitude, energy, and outcome. Encourage others to try it as you may encounter them in difficult circumstances. Share your stories of success with them.

RUNNING FAST

Life doesn't have to move as fast all the time. Look for and invite moments to slow down. At times, sacrifices have to be made, but in certain situations, it's worth it. Get creative, think outside the box, and look for ways to pace yourself.

DOES IT HAVE TO BE LIKE THIS?

You are needed and wanted. Preserve your well-being. Take care of yourself physically. Pull together a safe network of people to support you and who can give you the love and attention you deserve. Stay healthy!

FAITH OVER FEAR

Sometimes it's a blessing in disguise when we are forced to relinquish control and let things play out naturally. You save energy and often things work out for the best. Look for those opportunities as you go throughout your day.

ONE SELF-LOVE RULE

Write one of your self-love rules.

_____
_____
_____
_____
_____

MARCH

Living in Michigan, I always feel like a champion in the month of March. "I've survived another winter" is my celebratory stance at this point in the year. You can start to see the light at the end of a long, dark, cold, wintry tunnel. Who needs March Madness when you victoriously resurface at the top of your bracket from months of hibernation? March ushers in a sense of hope for me. I think for those in education, it could do the same. We've turned the corner; we are on the final stretch. The end is in sight.

I think about my brother-in-law who is a triathlete. He's completed several Ironman races. Think about the images of people as they cross the finish line. Some look tired but strong, while others can barely make those last steps, maybe even crawling across it. I'm sure there are a myriad of scientific reasons for those various degrees of completion. How well did they train? Did they pace themselves effectively? Did they hydrate appropriately? What was their nutrition before and during the race? Nevertheless, to me, there are a couple of takeaways: regardless of how haggard the finisher may look, they finished! And that's the goal! Get to the end! What are things you can do preemptively to ensure you have the strongest finish possible? I hope these March lessons will offer ideas on how to do just that.

5 Easy Tips for Living S.L.O.W.

There is talk about the importance of self-care. Regardless of your profession, if you aren't mindful and committed to monitoring your stress level and taking time to replenish and refresh, you can burn out! This is a common condition for those in the "helping others" professions. My goal is to offer suggestions for ways that you can take care of yourself.

In this book, these are ideas and strategies I've integrated into my hectic days to remind me to go SLOW; be mindful, present and positive about myself and others and to look for the good around me. I do not intend them to replace other, perhaps more complex, modes of care.

1. **Use jewelry** – I have a couple different pieces of jewelry I wear, depending on the situation. I inherited my grandmother's wedding ring, so on days when I feel like I need a little extra dose of love, I put that on and take a part of her with me. My son wears a woven bracelet he got while working in Haiti. All of these items can be touchstones for the day and prompts to stay focused on good. Perhaps you could find a touch stone too.
2. **Use clothing** - I'm sure you've heard the saying, "Put your big girl panties on" or "Put on your big boy pants." Keeping that in mind, I have a Wonder Woman T-shirt that serves me well on super stressful days.
3. **Use words** - I've learned some mantras through various Oprah and Deepak Chopra meditations. They can be very beneficial. I've also heard and use the phrase "All is well and all will be well." Sometimes, I have to consciously choose to believe that because there are times I don't feel like it's true.
4. **Use music** - It's amazing how music can change our mood. This is a definite go-to for me. Let me also say, there are other times I need silence, no music, just me and quiet space. I really try to be aware of what I need and use that time for myself.
5. **Use moments** - The next time you are in a waiting room or an airport gate or some "holding place," read or watch people or sit in silence and catch your breath. Notice people around you and send them love and peace, and/or count your blessings.

REFLECTIONS

1) Which of these 5 tips do you already use for your own self-care?

_____
_____
_____
_____
_____
_____

2) How well is it working?

_____
_____
_____
_____
_____
_____

3) Is there another one that you could try?

_____
_____
_____
_____
_____
_____

4) Is there something that isn't listed here that works well for you?

_____
_____
_____
_____
_____
_____

Prioritizing You Doesn't Bode Well For Me

The last couple of years, the flu season has been out of control. It can really take you out, the body aches, fever, chills, sinus congestion and coughing, low energy, no stamina. It is not pretty. Neither is the other "disease" I've coined the "Caregivers Curse." Its symptoms are somewhat similar to the flu - low energy, no stamina, and/or limited motivation.

As an "in-recovery codependent" I am starting to become astute in detecting these symptoms in myself and beginning to see them in others. This lesson comes down to this, when I prioritize someone other than myself it doesn't bode well for me. Putting others' needs ahead of your own is sometimes necessary but having that consume the way you live can have negative effects.

Life and the people in our lives can be demanding. It can feel like we are being pulled in a million directions with expectations and deadlines piling up all around us. This happens in our personal and professional lives. It may feel impossible to put yourself first when the ungraded papers are flying, and family members are calling and emails are buzzing. But I'm here to tell you it can be done. Prioritize you. See your value and stick to it.

I have found as I've been testing this theory and practicing setting boundaries that when I take a moment to step away from what seems like a situation that "only I" can resolve, I am able to find another solution that doesn't involve me.

When I step back it allows for others to step up. This means, while I'm growing in self-care others are growing personally as well. Perhaps really what I should really be saying instead is "prioritizing you doesn't bode well for me....or you". Whether it's eliminating the Caregivers Curse or keeping your house germ-free from the flu, keep washing your hands, covering your cough in our elbows, and putting yourself first. Here's to a healthy you!

REFLECTIONS

Write about a time when you put someone else's needs above your own and then you suffered for it.

Notes:
_____
_____
_____
_____

How could you have responded in that situation differently?

Notes:
_____
_____
_____
_____

What would have happened if you prioritized yourself?

Notes:
_____
_____
_____
_____

Take Back Your Power

I recently ordered a pair of Wonder Woman undies for a friend who is going through a hard time in her personal life. I think that everyone could probably benefit from a pair of Superhero underwear since no one is immune to difficult times in life.

I have been through times when things have been compounded for me, personal hurdles and work demands. Not only is it depleting but I find that I also start to feel inadequate and insecure.

Fortunately, I have people around me who can not only relate but reassure and guide me during those times. During those moments it's been beneficial for me to go SLOW and take time to reflect on past successes. Who do you have that can serve that same purpose for you? Utilize those confidants to help you bookmark ways that you have historically and successfully used the strengths and abilities embedded in you to rise above. Have them remind you of your power.

My encouragement to you is when things feel heavy and you feel powerless to overcome all that lies ahead, to not only go SLOW and take things step by step but to remember who you are and all you have to offer. Tap into your reservoir of talents and skills that make you, you. You have the power to make a difference in your life and, ultimately, in the lives of others. You can choose to be a robot or to be a Superhero. Pull up those undies of greatness and take back your power!

REFLECTIONS

Think about all the talents you possess. What would you say is your superpower? What are you really good at?

_____
_____
_____
_____
_____
_____
_____
_____

When do you feel at your strongest, physically and emotionally? When are you the most confident?

_____
_____
_____
_____
_____
_____
_____
_____
_____
_____
_____

Charged Up

My sister and I went to Florida to sell our dad's house and his beloved '50th edition Corvette. It's a beauty! It had all the bells and whistles and was kept in an insulated garage, driven once a week and had a trickle charger so the battery would not die. So imagine our surprise when we found the car was dead! We discovered the trickle charger had been moved to the other side of the garage and was not connected to the car. That'll do it.

Of course, we all know the importance of keeping our phones, laptops and other devices charged. I see people hovering around outlets at airports all the time, and often I am one of them. My motto is "plug in while you can." I was talking on my phone and as it was about to die, it, along with my dad's car, reinforced in me the importance of chargers and how much we depend on them. However, it also made me notice, that we don't necessarily take advantage of those same charging opportunities for ourselves.

There are numerous situations we face daily that can drain our battery, lowering our energy level. Emails, texts, phone calls, deadlines, requests, to name a few. But often we don't prioritize ourselves. What about your energy level? Where is your trickle charger? Is it connected? Or is it on the other side of the garage? I encourage you to notice your own personal battery life. What percentage are you on? Are there ways you can conserve energy? Can you go into "power saving mode"? What can you do to recharge?

We get to decide how much of our own battery we use up in our lives. It is ok to plug in or unplug and recharge. It is ok to put yourself first and take some down time. Look for your trickle charger, connect to it and watch your energy come back to life. You'll be zooming down the road, just like that gorgeous Corvette in no time.

REFLECTIONS

Read the below statements and check the ones that apply to you.

- I have what I need to recharge my batteries.

- I know ways to recharge my battery.

- I never let my battery run too low.

- My battery is always hovers near five percent.

- I don't panic when my battery runs low.

- I know when to unplug and when to recharge.

Notes:
_____
_____
_____
_____

Good For You

At a True Colors© workshop, I learned that I am very clearly a Gold, especially at work. These workshops help you identify your personality type by color. In short, Golds, like me, are structured. We like everything to be in order, notoriously make lists and are focused on checking things off those lists. As a Gold, I am drawn to other Golds.

Several of my co-workers, a couple of whom also happen to be Golds, experienced some challenging life situations. With each circumstance we were able to support one another. We covered for one another, stood in the work gap and freely gave permission to step away and reprioritize. There was grace and flexibility. It made me wonder then why it seems so natural to give grace to others but then neglect to extend that same quality to ourselves.

The same can be said for taking time off work. I've noticed how congratulatory we are for others who go on vacation but then hesitate to allow ourselves a hard-earned reprieve. The unstated yet expected work culture across the country in many fields, including education, seems to be one of "don't stop till you drop."

My hope is that we can begin to shift our mindsets around our priorities, not just individually but within the educational system and perhaps even eventually as a culture, and learn to stick to our values. In every self-care training I conduct, we talk about values and without fail, every.single.time. "health" and "family" are some of the first ones shared. Granted, for the Golds of the world, hard-work and the sense of accomplishment are also highly valued, but so are our health and family.

If we could collectively attempt to start reinforcing decisions with one another and personally, to not stay late at work, to enjoy downtime over the weekend, to praise full nights of sleep, perhaps we can move towards genuine expressions of "Good for You" not just for others but for ourselves as well.

REFLECTIONS

Think about a time when you decided not to over-extend yourself. Perhaps you left work on time or didn't work over the weekend. How did you feel?

_____
_____
_____
_____
_____
_____
_____
_____

What, if any, negative repercussions were there? What were the positives?

_____
_____
_____
_____
_____
_____
_____
_____
_____
_____
_____

S.L.O.W. ROAD RULES

LIVING SLOW TIPS

Consider sharing your "works well" tip with a colleague or friend. Swapping ideas with others is a great way to encourage collective well-being and as well as getting new strategies for yourself.

PRIORITIZING YOU IS BAD FOR ME

Sometimes it's better for everyone involved if we step back and let others figure things out for themselves. It's an opportunity for them to learn and grow and for us to protect our energy reserves.

TAKE BACK YOUR POWER

Remember to hold on to our strengths, especially in challenging times. They can potentially give us the boost we need to persevere. Carry them with pride and confidence as you go day to day.

CHARGED UP

I love that our phones denote the percentage of battery life, as I am often monitoring it. We have that gauge as well if we pay attention to it. Look for signs that you need to go into "power saving mode" and switch into that gear as indicated.

GOOD FOR YOU

It can be difficult to retrain yourself out of the "always working" mode. Maybe there are some feelings of guilt that rise up. That is to be expected, but it is ok to stop the train sometimes. In fact, it's necessary. Look for those opportunities, they are there.

ONE SELF-LOVE RULE

Write one of your self-love rules.

APRIL

Its April and spring is in the air! As flowers and trees start blooming, nature adds more delightful color and activity back into the world. The daylight hours begin to last longer and there is a sense of renewal as winter ends and a new season begins. I love fresh starts! It's so nice to have opportunities for "do overs." I appreciate when people show me grace, and I try to offer it to others as well. Like Maya Angelou said, "When we know better, we do better."

We all need and deserve those chances to learn and grow. As we evolve in our ability to attend to our own needs and well-being, it's helpful to be reminded of ways to do just that. The April lessons remind us to be honest with ourselves and others, to be intentional about going step by step, and to stay in our own lane. These are practices that can improve our own welfare.

Honesty is the Best Policy

It may come as a surprise to some, but there are days when I'm in a funk! I call it being prickly. If I was in "one of those moods" and had to get in front of a classroom of students, it could prove challenging, especially if the students are also in "one of those moods." I hope this lesson can help provide an approach or perspective to ease what might become an even worse day.

First, "fake it to make it" may seem like a viable technique on occasion, but kids can usually tell if you're faking it. As a mental health professional, I suggest you consider an alternative option - allow yourself to feel and acknowledge your emotions, then address them. This could help improve things for you and those around you, and avoid unforeseen or brewing emotional disruptions.

Approaching your classroom with honesty and vulnerability, even on "funk" days, can be beneficial. Share your good days with your class - "I'm excited to see you guys!"; and be truthful about your bad days too - "I'm so overwhelmed today." Consider disclosing why you're not at your best if appropriate. What do you think would happen? It's true that some students will take advantage of you when you're vulnerable. However, it is also a great chance to model healthy emotional regulation and trust. This strategy demonstrates that you are self-aware, can self-manage, and are, wait for it... human too!

Try asking for extra cooperation and understanding from your class on hard days. Asking for what you need provides a good example for them around self-awareness and relationship building skills. It shows them how to express their feelings and needs in a constructive way and to look to others for support. Kids possess strength, resilience, and the capacity to love and care. When given the chance, they can be a source of comfort and support.

Finally, let your students know when you are doing better. Show them how things improved or what you did to make a change. Empower them to follow suit and the environment in the room and the outcome of the day will be more productive and pleasant. Try it, see how it goes.

REFLECTIONS

1) What happened during a time when you were not honest about your feelings?

_____
_____
_____
_____
_____
_____

2) What happened during a time when you were honest about how you felt?

_____
_____
_____
_____
_____
_____

3) How did those two situations compare?

_____
_____
_____
_____
_____
_____

4) How did they impact you?

_____
_____
_____
_____
_____

One Step at a Time

As I prepare this lesson on taking things "one step at a time," I'm watching news coverage of the March for Our Lives movement. I'm inspired by the young people marching for change and the adult support they've received. As a social worker, I'm naturally drawn to events that help empower and advocate for those without a voice. This has been my mission in life, fighting for a better way of life for all. It fills my heart with hope, and I'm encouraged by such a united front.

Change like this can be daunting, but it is often incremental and starts with small steps. Heading into March, I had my own "March Madness" experience with loads of meetings, presentations and trainings to conduct. As my anxiety levels rose, I knew it was time to implement self-care strategies to stay sane and healthy.

In my work with educators, I know that feeling is all too familiar. Educators face high demands, increasing needs, and have limited resources. With security threats on the rise, how can teachers teach and students learn? It's a stressful and disconcerting environment for both students and teachers. The only solution is taking it "one step at a time" - facing hard times with courage and awareness, and practicing self-care strategies to maintain safety and wellness.

Through this last month, when I started to think about all that was facing me, I could sense my stress increasing, so I would take a deep breath and tell myself, "One step at a time" or "Day by day" or "Step by step;" "Don't get ahead of yourself, focus on today." It really helped! Additionally, I made a list of dates and events I had in March. I would check them off that list in the evening as I got through each one. That practice gave me a sense of relief and accomplishment. I also was strategic about scheduling in some self-care by planning dinner and hang time with friends, going to the movies and scheduling a massage. These moments kept me refreshed as I made my way through the month. Using those strategies and mantras made a difference for me as I got through my "March Madness" and so I share them with you in hopes that as you feel overwhelmed with all you have to do, you too can SLOW down and take things One. Step. At. A. Time.

REFLECTIONS

WHEN THINGS PILE UP FOR YOU WHAT IS A STRATEGY YOU USE TO GET THROUGH THAT HECTIC TIME?

A. _____ C. _____

B. _____ D _____

HOW DO YOU PLAN TO GO STEP BY STEP THROUGH A BUSY SCHEDULE?

A. _____ C. _____

B. _____ D _____

DOES IT HELP TO ALLEVIATE STRESS?

A. YES   B   NO

C. EXPLAIN_____

_____

_____

BASED ON THE READING ABOVE, WHAT ARE SOME OTHER THINGS YOU CAN TRY?

A. _____ C. _____

B. _____ D _____

Stay in Your Lane

Research tells us that teachers, along with emergency room nurses, are in a career with the highest stress level, though other professionals also experience stress in their work environments.

Having problem-solving capabilities is advantageous as problem-solvers tend to be compassionate and passionate. This was a primary influencer in my decision to become a social worker, as I am passionate about making a difference and want to help other people. But, if I don't establish boundaries, it can be tricky as I default to a "fixer" and insert myself into everyone's problems. As I become more self-aware, I'm paying attention to my behavior in such scenarios and it inspired this month's lesson.

So how does this support self-care, you ask? Supporting self-care involves not offering or taking over solutions to others' problems, especially when they didn't ask me to do so. This prevents them from growing and learning from their own experiences as well as building their confidence in their own efficacy. I am, in essence, learning to stay in my lane.

In an effort to stay in my lane, I've begun to check in with myself in a couple of ways. My new rule of thumb is to consider if this person asked me for help or to get involved, in the first place? If not, perhaps they just need a supportive ear. The next question I ask myself is, does this involve me? Is it any of my business? Sometimes various circumstances can surface around me that really don't concern me and yet I am tempted to, and at times have, inserted myself. It's draining and unnecessary to be in the know all the time. Letting go of the need to control and influence situations has been freeing, and intentionally selecting what I focus on is liberating. As I release the need to be included, different and more invigorating uses of my time present themselves.

As always, I encourage you to try this approach for yourself. Use my two "check-in with yourself" questions or find what works well for you. No matter what you choose, I hope you stay healthy, safe and in your own lane.

REFLECTIONS

Read the below statements and check the ones that apply to you.

- I love being in control but find it exhausting.

- I don't like being left out of decisions concerning others.

- I feel great when others insert themselves into my work.

- I feel frustrated when others insert themselves into my work.

- I try to help others even when I'm not asked.

- I want to stay in my lane but find it challenging at times.

Notes:

_____

_____

_____

_____

Silver Linings

In 2020, it was impossible to avoid the difficult reality we were facing with the Covid19 pandemic. It was the primary focus of all news reports, social media posts, and daily conversations. As a school mental health consultant, my job entails supporting students' and educators' mental wellness and it was all consuming and compounded by those events.

It would have been natural and justified for any of us to feel anxious and stressed during that time of isolation, constraint, and limitation, however, during all the chaos, emotion and distress, I learned to reframe and find silver linings. This lesson reflects on that time.

For someone frequently on the road, it was a blessing in disguise to be "stuck" at home. I chose to take advantage of a few things and look for silver linings to help guide my decisions:

- I enjoyed the travel-free time - no suitcase to pack or arrangements to make.
- I didn't panic purchase and only got and used what I needed to sustain myself.
- I actually ate the food from the freezer and pantry and cooked a lot more.
- I connected more with my family and friends more through FaceTime, text, and phone calls.

Though it was a tough time, engaging in distanced relationships was a balm for the soul. It was refreshing to see the unity across the country, from streaming live workouts to learning about self-sacrifice and ingenuity. Teachers emailed to check in, car parades, food deliveries, and increased recognition for what educators and health care workers were doing on the front lines showed that we could pull together in troubled times. It filled my heart.

Then and now, I hope when times are uncertain we can fight to find morsels of goodness. We must always remember that in every hard time, there is always a silver lining. Let's continue to stay healthy, safe, and well.

REFLECTIONS

Do you recall the beginning of the pandemic? How have things changed since then?

_____
_____
_____
_____
_____
_____
_____
_____

What are lessons you've learned since April 2020? What are some of the blessings from that time till now?

_____
_____
_____
_____
_____
_____
_____
_____
_____
_____
_____

You are Not Alone

I saw this quote on social media, "The cure for burnout isn't and can't be self-care. It has to be all of us caring for each other" by Emily and Amelia Nagoski. Truthfully, at first pass I did not like the quote and I'm not sure I completely agree with it. However, I could modify it a little to say that "the cure for burnout isn't and can't *only* be about self-care. It has to include all of us caring for each other". In this last month, I've recognized even more the importance of "my village," thus the focus of this lesson.

During the pandemic and the last couple of years, I noticed a pattern in my work schedule, with October and March being especially busy. This March was no different, with lots of professional responsibilities like zoom presentations and meetings, plus a statewide SEL campaign. Meanwhile, "back at the ranch," there were things brewing on the home front as well. Isn't that often the case, when things pile up, they really pile up?

My family recently faced a traumatic situation, taking an emotional and physical toll on us. This made me realize the importance of seeking help and support from my "village." Despite my commitment to self-care moments, I had to admit Emily and Amelia were right: I couldn't do it alone. I was amazed at the responses when I asked for help; it reassured me that when you call the cavalry, they show up!

Think of a handful of folks in your village who would show up for you and vice versa. That my friends, is self-care. Knowing when you need the support, and then being vulnerable enough to ask for it! That is taking care of you!

I understand the hesitation to be open, but expressing your needs shouldn't feel that vulnerable. We should feel safe and it should be the norm to communicate our needs to those we trust. Self-care is about all of us doing our part to take care of ourselves ***and*** one another.

Identify those who are part of your village and who show up for you. Remember you are not alone!

REFLECTIONS

1) Identify four
reliable people in
your village?

⬤ _____   ⬤ _____

⬤ _____   ⬤ _____

2) Do you feel free
to ask for their
assistance when
you need it?

⬤ Sometimes   ⬤ Never

⬤ Always   ⬤ It depends

3) Do you allow
them to help you?

⬤ Yes   ⬤ Sometimes

⬤ No   ⬤ _____

4) What holds you
back, if anything?

⬤ Fear   ⬤ Pride

⬤ Anxiety   ⬤ Other_____

S.L.O.W. ROAD RULES

HONESTY IS THE BEST POLICY

Make a commitment to prioritize things in your life as part of your self-care. Identify one thing you can do for yourself today to help fill your cup. Then pick something for the next day. These should be small, easy things. Don't worry about the big picture–rather, just make a small commitment every day. Do it for a few days and see how it feels.

STAY IN YOUR LANE

As care-giving professionals, it can be easy to automatically step in to "help" others. Granted, sometimes is it helpful. Other times maybe not so much. Practice self-awareness, self-control and asking if/when help is needed and if you can be of service. Free up your time by staying in your lane.

STEP BY STEP

Make a list of small celebrations or breaks you can embed throughout a busy time in life. Coffee break with a friend, a 20-minute walk, a happy hour.

SILVER LININGS

It's easy to think about all of the negative, it's in front of us all the time. However, look for the rainbow after the storm. You may have to really search, and it may take time to find but often it is there. Hold on to the good.

YOU ARE NOT ALONE

It is hard to relinquish control sometimes. It feels easier when you have people you trust, know they have your back and are on the same page as you. It's ok to share your hesitation or reservation. It may actually help to reassure you to let go and let others. Its freeing to not have to carry the burden alone.

ONE SELF-LOVE RULE

Write one of your self-love rules.

QUARTERLY REVIEW

FEBRUARY - APRIL

BABY STEPS I TOOK

1 _____
2 _____
3 _____

PROUDEST MOMENTS

1 _____
2 _____
3 _____

HIGHLIGHTS

_____
_____
_____

LESSONS I LEARNED

_____
_____
_____

WHAT WORKED

_____
_____
_____
_____
_____
_____
_____

DO BETTER NEXT TIME

_____
_____
_____
_____
_____
_____
_____
_____

IMPROVEMENTS TO MAKE

_____
_____
_____
_____

QUARTERLY PREVIEW

MAY - JULY

THINKING AHEAD

BRIEF MOMENTS AHEAD

1
2
3

I'M EXCITED FOR

I'M CONCERNED ABOUT

MAIN GOALS

MAIN GOALS

IMPORTANT DATES

PART

living
S.L.O.W.™

5

SLIDE INTO SUMMER

Don't give up now! Look how far you've come! You're sliding into home stretch with a sense of accomplishment and headed towards rest and relaxation. This was likely a time of growth as you prioritized yourself and ended the year less frazzled. It's now time to reset and refresh. Use these summer months to focus on yourself, the things you love, and restore your energy - it's time to take care of you!

MAY
- Be Brave - Say What You Need
- Preventative Self-Care
- You Are What You Think
- Do What You Can
- It's Not Your Job

JUNE
- Caregiver's Curse
- Growing UP From Here
- Greater Joy Ahead
- Reset
- Reflections

JULY
- What Story Are You Telling Yourself?
- Time Is Your Friend
- Are You There Yet?
- Speak Your Truth
- Making Lemonade

First: Complete the assessment on the following page.

SUMMER ASSESSMENT

		YES	NO
1	I have self-care tools at my disposal that I can maximize during this time.	☐	☐
2	I was helpful to my colleagues this past school year.	☐	☐
3	There were things that worked well in class this past year and I will do them again.	☐	☐
4	There were things that didn't work well this past year and I know what they are.	☐	☐
5	I definitely grew professionally this past year thanks to my self-care practices.	☐	☐
6	I know which colleagues are the most helpful to my educational and self-care journey.	☐	☐
7	This past year was stressful and frustrating.	☐	☐
8	I have at least three healthy ways to relieve stress this coming school year.	☐	☐

NOTES

NOTES

MAY

One thing I have recognized as I continue to practice my own self-care and talk to others about theirs is how much of it is really about having self-awareness and courage. We often operate on autopilot, missing out on opportunities to prioritize our well-being. The good news is that even small moments of self-care can have a positive impact. Look for those chances throughout the day and make the most of them.

I used to stay so busy and unaware that if you asked me, "what do you need right now?" I would have looked at you as if you were speaking in a foreign language. I still have to slow down to check in with myself, but I've gotten much better at being aware of those needs.

The next hurdle is once you recognize your needs, it's time to communicate them. This can feel intimidating, so you have to find the courage to get it out. You might feel pretty vulnerable, as it's hard to verbalize your needs to yourself, let alone to someone else. I encourage you to practice in safe spaces with safe people who will reinforce and reassure you. It gets easier with time. Just like building muscle, repetition helps. I hope these blogs written in May help you flex that muscle.

Be Brave

I've been observing a trend in conversations I've been having lately. Most notably, I was astonished at a female adolescent's capability to express what she needs in a disagreement with a friend. She wanted open, honest communication and closure. This made me think about how it took me until my 30's to understand this concept, and I'm still mastering it. Add to that, a colleague was hesitant about a business opportunity. Instead of jumping in, she expressed her reservations and asked for what she needed to feel good about it. The organization was responsive, and it looks like it will be a good prospect. I love that the universe honors us when we speak up.

Growing up, I was conditioned to put others' needs before my own. Expressing my needs felt selfish, and it took me a long time to recognize and communicate them. Now, I'm practicing saying what I need, as it's essential for my self-care journey. Can you relate?

Focusing on others instead of ourselves can be a tempting distraction, but, as a therapist once told me, "Our feelings won't be denied." Ignoring our needs can lead to emotional or physical distress. I, for one, dislike being sick. I'm assuming you do as well. It is okay to say no, take a break, or ask for help. Lyrics from Sara Bareilles song Brave comes to mind:

"Say what you wanna say
And let the words fall out
Honestly, I want to see you be brave."

Taking a stand for yourself requires courage, but it gets easier with practice. I've learned to pause and check in with my needs, even if it's just taking a minute to think before responding. This stops me from simply complying with everyone else's expectations.

I hope you can continue being "Brave" and taking care of yourself, so you are whole enough to help those around you.

REFLECTIONS

1) Reflect on a time that you spoke up for yourself. What were the circumstances around that situation?

_____
_____
_____
_____
_____

2) Was it easy or hard for you to speak up? What motivated you to do it?

_____
_____
_____
_____
_____

3) How did it go? Did it work well?

_____
_____
_____
_____
_____

4) What did you learn from that experience?

_____
_____
_____
_____
_____

Preventative Self-Care

I have had some meaningful conversations about self-care. Obviously, that is something I talk about frequently, as it is one of my passions and those around me know that. But I mean really, intentionally taking care of yourSELF. Throughout these discussions, I noticed that recurring theme.

What I noticed and am paying extra attention to now is more about what we could call preventative self-care. It's thinking about ways to preserve yourself, your energy, your well-being in your day-to-day life. Is it possible to make choices as you go throughout your day that allow you to maintain some self-care, so you aren't so depleted when your head hits the pillow at night? Can you establish some boundaries to conserve energy? Or can you try to be more in tune with what you need as you go throughout the day?

I am making it more of a precedence to deliberately think through how I want to spend my time each day. I am also very aware that some of us may not have the luxury to put off some tasks. Or we may not think we have that luxury? What I am learning about myself and others is that we are adept at turning molehills into mountains. We can get overwhelmed with the thought of being overwhelmed.

Frequently, people are much more gracious with their expectations of me than I am of myself. I encourage you to adopt that gracious approach for yourSELF. Perhaps if we SLOW down, take a breath and a step back, things aren't really as daunting as they seem. This is when my mom's saying comes to mind "Do not borrow tomorrow's worries today."

I'm hoping as we continue to tackle our ever-growing to-do list, we can keep our thoughts, feelings, and needs in the forefront. Intentionally decide what is okay and reasonable for you to do, what someone else can do, or if it can wait. I plan to be mindful and aware of choices I make to do some preventative SELF-care. You should too!

REFLECTIONS

THINK ABOUT AND WRITE DOWN THE BUSIEST TIMES OF THE YEAR FOR YOU. IS THERE A PATTERN?

HOW DO YOU FEEL AS THOSE TIMES GET NEARER?

A. EXCITED   C. ANXIOUS
B. EXHAUSTED   D   FRUSTRATED

HOW DO YOU FEEL AT THE END OF THOSE PERIODS?

A. RELIEVED   C. HAPPY
B. EXHAUSTED   D   FRUSTRATED

WHAT CAN YOU DO TO BETTER PREPARE FOR THEM, SO YOU AREN'T AS TIRED AT THE END?

A. _____   C. _____
B. _____   D   _____

You Are What You Think

The statement "you are what you eat" is commonly accepted. People understand that if you eat a bunch of junk, chances are you will not be healthy and/or fit (although I know a few who are, for whatever reason, exempt from that truth and I am jealous!). The point behind that belief is that what you put in your body makes a difference. Input can equal or impact output. Thus, to me, the premise holds true for our minds and our bodies. What we put into our minds can alter what we believe about ourselves, or how we feel about ourselves, or even how we behave based on those thoughts.

With this perspective in mind, over the last month, I've done a little experimenting and "research." I have paid attention to what I say to myself and how that affects my demeanor and behavior. I've also watched those around me, noticing those same factors. I experienced people, self-included, communicate, "I am so busy." Or "I am so tired." Or "I am so stressed." Only to find out as those statements were further investigated, that there really wasn't much merit to them.

Regardless of whether life is genuinely busy and stressful, or we just say it is, my first encouragement is for us to be more mindful about what we communicate to others. Think before we speak. However, the main point of this lesson is to also then be aware of not only what we say to others but what we say to ourselves.

Over the years, I have had many conversations with young women who are wrestling with feelings of insecurity. "I'm not as pretty as the other girls". "I'm never going to pass this test." "I can't speak in front of other people." "He's the best and only guy that will ever like me." Those false lines we tell ourselves don't benefit us. They are harmful and can infiltrate the good that lies within us. They overshadow the truth of all we possess and can impede us from blossoming into our fullest potential.

My hope is that all of us can not only see our value but believe it, feel it, be convinced of it, and allow that belief to propel us forward. Think the best about yourself because you are what you think.

REFLECTIONS

Imagine you are with a group of family and friends. They are celebrating you. What are the things they say about you in celebration? Are you loyal? Funny? Honest? Kind?

_____
_____
_____
_____
_____
_____
_____
_____

Of those compliments, what stands out to you the most? Write down 3 things you love about yourself. Maybe they are the same things or maybe they are different.

_____
_____
_____
_____
_____
_____
_____
_____
_____
_____
_____

Do What You Can

A couple of years ago, a friend of mine sent me a quote that says, "Start where you are. Use what you have. Do what you can." I have it hanging up in my office and refer to it often, either as my own personal reminder or to impart it to someone else.

Initially, as things were shutting down because of the Coronavirus, and our leaders encouraged us to stay home to "flatten the curve," I saw it as an opportunity to go SLOW. I didn't realize how drastically things were going to shift for educators. It was impressive to see the efforts made by so many teachers. I saw them working tirelessly to connect with students, ensuring their emotional well-being while also stabilizing and enriching their academic achievements. What I thought was going to be an opportunity to move forward at a more reasonable pace became yet another break-neck race, complicated by various limitations, including attending to personal familial needs and priorities, along with many emotions: fear, anxiety, grief, that are bound to be felt at this time.

I encouraged educators to feel their feelings, as those were uncertain times with no end in sight. We also experienced a lot of grief, such as loss of loved ones, lost freedom, and milestone celebrations. It was okay to be sad and take the time to mourn those things. Many educators cried, journaled, and gave themselves permission to feel and share their feelings without judgment.

These days, as I connect with educators across the state and nation, my encouragement to them is the same. "Do what you can." That's all that can and should be expected. I now deliberately communicate with colleagues when I'm logging off work and shifting my focus to family and fun. It is okay to establish boundaries and prioritize your own health and well-being. We will be forever changed because of that historic time. I just hope as we re-set that our commitment to only "do what we can" stays with us unapologetically. Stay safe and be well!

REFLECTIONS

Read the below statements and check the ones that apply to you.

- I find it easy to only do what I can.

- Even if it's frustrating, I have to do more than expected.

- I feel like a failure if something is left undone.

- I find it easy to set work boundaries.

- I find it hard to set work boundaries.

- I often apologize if I can't do more than is expected.

Notes:
_____
_____
_____
_____

It's Not Your Job

After I was fully vaccinated, I visited my father and was glad to see him in person. He told me about a woman at his residence he had befriended. He had been helping her in her wheelchair to dinner, but was told by the medical staff that this was preventing her from building up her own strength and ability to manage on her own. Her need for a wheelchair was meant to be temporary. That story resonated with me.

How many times do we see a need and jump right in to help meet it? Please hear me correctly. I'm not saying we don't ever volunteer to help someone in need, especially someone who depends on us. What I am saying is for us to be more deliberate and discerning before making that move. Consider, if I always did my children's laundry. As they matured, they would never learn to do it themselves.

It can be the same thing with our students, or coworkers, or even our own friends and family. As hard as it may be to see those we care about struggling, sometimes, it is just what they may need to learn and grow to become their own best self. Reflect on your own experiences with difficult times. Think about ways they made you stronger, more resilient, more self-assured in the end. You came through those challenges, perhaps a little bruised and battered, but you are arguably better off. We should want to provide those same learning opportunities for others. Maybe we offer our lessons learned to help people avoid some of the same mistakes. And we can provide words of reassurance, comfort, or encouragement, but it's impossible to protect everyone from every hurtful scenario. And it's not our job.

We each have our own responsibility to "fix", care, and nurture ourselves. Use your energy to fill your cup, to ensure you are healthy and well. Walk alongside of your friend, but don't push them, especially if they need to learn to walk on their own again. Give them the time and space to get back on their feet while you work to stay on yours. In time, with kindness, patience and support, we can all walk together again in strength.

REFLECTIONS

Reflect back on a time you learned a hard but life-changing lesson. What was it?

_____
_____
_____
_____
_____
_____
_____
_____

What did you learn? How have you benefited from that experience?

_____
_____
_____
_____
_____
_____
_____
_____
_____
_____

S.L.O.W. ROAD RULES

BE BRAVE

There are times that are easier than others to advocate for ourselves. Depending on the situation, who we are communicating with and why, and what we are hoping to gain from the conversation can impact our courage to speak up. It does take bravery. It's okay to practice this skill with trusted friends first. Try it!

PREVENTATIVE SELF-CARE

Being pre-emptive as we head into busy times can be helpful. We monitor the weather so we can be prepared. We should do that for our own wellness too. Build up your reserves.

YOU ARE WHAT YOU THINK

What good things have people said about you? Think about those accolades. Hold on to them. Carry them with you in confidence and with pride. You deserve to feel good and believe the best about yourself. You are worth it! You can do it!

DO WHAT YOU CAN

We grow stronger through hard times. Remember that you are a champion! You've overcome some of the most trying times in our history. Carry with you the confidence that you can do it. You've done it before. You are resilient!

IT'S NOT YOUR JOB

Life-changing lessons are not usually fun as they're happening. But often, we are better on the other side as a result. Allow others to have their own experience to learn and grow. Practice resisting the urge to always help, especially if it takes away from others growth opportunity.

ONE SELF-LOVE RULE

Write one of your self-love rules.

JUNE

Welcome to my favorite month! I LOVE June! To me, it signifies the official beginning of summer, which is my favorite season. I love the longer, warm days. There is a carefree sense in the air. And in Michigan, it's the end of the school year! This also contributes to the feeling of being carefree.

When my kids were in school, I loved the freedom that came from the end of the school year. No more lunches to pack, or homework assignments to complete, no policing bedtime routines. Freedom! Additionally, and maybe even a bit selfishly, it is also my favorite because it's my birthday month. I have friends who don't particularly like to celebrate their birthday. They would prefer to keep the aging clock at bay, but I don't mind it so much. I get excited about all the goodness a new year of life will bring. I anticipate "the future". I work to be a better version of myself each year. It feels fulfilling. Another opportunity to take another shot. Like activities common to making New Year's resolutions, I use this chance to be reflective. What have I learned in the last year? What are my plans for the next year?

You will sense my reflection as you read through the June lessons that follow. I use circumstances and experiences to evolve and grow into a better version of myself. I hope these lessons help you do the same.

Caregiver's Curse

As a mental health professional and social worker, it's easy to neglect my own well-being while caring for others. When I don't take the time to check in with myself, I become drained & of no help to anyone. It's hard to understand the importance of putting my own needs first, especially because I get value and worth from helping others. I'm sure I'm not alone in this. I will also propose that this is more common for women than men, as society often socializes us this way.

I call this the Caregiver's Curse. It's when you feel responsible for everyone, their happiness and health, before thinking about your own needs. You tell yourself that "everyone is counting on you" and/or "what would they do without you" and/or "there is no one else to take care of this", the rationalizations go on and on.

After decades of neglecting my own needs, I began a self-improvement journey in my late 30's and early 40's after a mini emotional breakdown and awakening. I now realize that I have a choice. I believe it's vital to establishing healthy boundaries, so here are some of my go to statements that help me do just that.

1. *"Oh I'd love to help you with X,Y,Z. Here's when I'm available and how much time I have."* Give only as much as you can AFFORD to give.
2. That works for phone calls too, something like, *"I only have 10 minutes to talk because I have a few other things I need to get done today."* Set time limits.
3. *"Oh, XYZ happened to you?! Oh! I'm sorry to hear this, what are you going to do?"* This is one I use often with those who may want me to fix the problem.
4. *"Oh, XYZ happened? Yikes! That's hard (or sad or too bad)! I'll keep you in my thoughts/prayers."* I am notorious for carrying other people's burdens.

I hope that as you move forward, you are able to set some limits. Really consider how much you take on, releasing yourself from the responsibility of taking care of everyone before taking care of you. Break the Caregivers Curse. It's okay to say no sometimes. Remember you have a choice!

REFLECTIONS

1) Think about the people who depend on you. Who are they?

_____   _____

_____   _____

2) What do you do for them?

_____   _____

_____   _____

3) What can they do for themselves?

_____   _____

_____   _____

4) What are ways you can start to let go and allow them to take some responsibility?

_____
_____
_____
_____
_____

Growing Up From Here

A few years ago, my son had a close call with death. While in the hospital, I read an article on Post Traumatic Growth. I shared this article with my son, which gave us a sense of hope that we could learn and grow from the grueling experience. With time, we were able to reframe our experience and see the strength and resilience it brought us. Then, in a recent conversation with a friend, we were reminiscing about how we met and how our lives have changed over the years of our friendship. We reflected on our various career paths. Some were great experiences and others not so much, but even in those less-than-ideal circumstances, we learned so much. It reminded me of the Post Traumatic Growth article. That even when things in life or work are difficult and stressful, we can gain so much if we SLOW down and take the time to notice and learn.

An important and probably obvious lesson we can glean from those situations is learning what we don't want. Establishing boundaries is crucial to defining this in our lives. We need to be mindful of our personal limits and set expectations accordingly. Think of a water pump with a floater. The floater triggers when it reaches a certain point and releases pressure. It's essential for us to determine our own personal floater trigger point.

Besides learning what we don't want, we can learn what we do want and what we are made of. We can learn from our hardships and gain strength, confidence, resilience to forge new paths. Knowing who to rely on during hard times is key. Symbolisms like diamonds coming from coal or the phoenix rising from the ashes may be overused, but they remind us we can become our best selves and grow through difficult times.

As the school year nears its end, it's a time for reflection. We may be exhausted and looking forward to the end of homework and lunches, but we should also celebrate our successes and the ways we have grown. Have you been able to pace yourself and build in self-care? Have you developed resilience and established boundaries? Use your summer to revitalize and refresh your mind with a plan.

REFLECTIONS

Unfortunately, most of us can probably think of a personal traumatic experience. Reflect on that situation and consider the ways you've grown. How did that experience change you?

_____
_____
_____
_____
_____
_____
_____

What do you do differently now? Do you respond to others more graciously? Are you more gracious with yourself? How are you better because of it?

_____
_____
_____
_____
_____
_____
_____
_____
_____
_____
_____

Greater Joy Ahead

I've been contemplating what would be beneficial for us to think about as the end of the school year approaches. This is usually an extremely busy time for schools, staff, students, and families. There is the end of year push to finish the curriculum, wrap up classes, and get grading done. In addition to all the extra stress teachers are facing, student behaviors at this time in the school year typically magnify. The weather is warmer, summer break is nearing, and students get antsy. Everyone is ready to be done and is looking forward to a change in pace.

In the last month or so, I have felt it and I'm learning that it's okay to feel my feelings. Sometimes, I need permission from my closest friends to be upset and emotional. My mom says, "feel your feelings, and think your thoughts, but don't think your feelings." That is sound advice. During those times, processing through journaling or talking with a trusted confidant works wonders; then, I decompress by taking a walk, running, or riding my bike. What things that work for you? Is it painting, coloring, reading or hitting a punching bag? To get to a place of peace and calm, do what helps you get there.

Finally, once I have worked through what I am feeling and I'm able to think more calmly and logically, I can often see the good in those situations. I am a believer that nothing in your life has to be wasted. Things happen for a reason, and when I pay attention, I learn from even the most difficult, emotional, and frustrating situations.

I encourage you to feel your feelings and then find the silver lining in all situations. No matter how challenging they may be, there's always a reason to be grateful. As you race to the end of this school year, I hope you'll see the good things and experiences around you and then head into summer with even greater joy.

REFLECTIONS

WHEN ARE YOU THE HAPPIEST?

WHAT BRINGS YOU JOY?

A. _____ C. _____

B. _____ D _____

WHAT DO YOU LOOK FORWARD TO?

CAN YOU THINK OF LITTLE PLEASURES THAT PRESENT THEMSELVES TO YOU THROUGHOUT YOUR DAY? WHAT ARE THOSE THINGS? REALLY BE REFLECTIVE.

Reset

I am a firm believer that everything happens for a reason. I choose to believe that good comes from bad. I am the type of person who looks for "the lesson." Why is this happening? What can I gain from this experience? During the pandemic, I fought to hold on to that belief.

As many states began to re-open, I saw it as an opportunity for all of us to reset, realign, and re-establish our priorities. Ideally, we would reset globally, politically, and nationally. I would have been thrilled if there was a reset academically. As we moved to online learning, did you notice the shift to just focus on the basics? Teachers checked in with every student, making sure they were safe and secure. Did they need food or emotional support? That became their emphasis. Permission to lighten the academic expectations, including no achievement tests and modified AP tests, was given. We paid attention to the humanity of students, their families, and educators. Could we carry that forward in the coming months?

I'm not so sure anyone realized my grandiose wishes for a complete overhaul of our established systems, but if nothing else, perhaps we reset personally. What changes did you make and have continued: Have you taken more time to get outside? Taken more walks? Become more physically active? Spent more time with family? Reached out to friends more often and in innovative ways? Developed new hobbies?

Just like iron is refined with fire, so is our human nature. When push comes to shove, many of us rally. We come together, adjust, rise to the occasion, and come out on the other side stronger and better. Remember that time and commit to using the lessons learned. Take advantage of your reset!

REFLECTIONS

1) When is a time you wanted a do-over?

_____
_____
_____
_____
_____
_____

2) What happened in that situation?

_____
_____
_____
_____
_____

3) If you could go back, what would you have done differently?

_____
_____
_____
_____
_____

4)What is something you have the power to change now?

_____
_____
_____
_____
_____

Reflections

June is one of my favorite months of the year for a couple of reasons. First of all, to me, it represents the first month of summer. I remember as a young child relishing the end of the school year. Secondly, as previously indicated, it's my birthday month. I love birthdays! Typically, the weeks leading up to my birthday are reflective for me. This year, I thought it may be beneficial to share some of the realizations I've been contemplating recently. Perhaps some of them with resonate with you. Here are some of my reflections.

Relationships serve a purpose. Sometimes connections with others can be for just a season or a reason. Not all relationships are life-long and that's okay. There are relationships that come and go. Perhaps they were temporary to teach a brief lesson or to bring reprieve or an awareness of a need and then they depart after they've done their job. Finally, there are relationships that fall in between and are on a continuum. Each of these contribute to who we are and who we become.

Pick your battles. As I get older, I'm becoming more discerning about how to spend my energy. In my younger years, especially as a social worker I wanted to fight every fight and inserted myself in situations around me even if it only involved me indirectly. I've learned there are boundaries you can set to save your energy. It's hard to do at times, but the payoff is worth it.

Kindness matters. Remember the saying "If you don't have anything nice to say...?" I'm seeing that over and over in our society. Putting positive energy out into the world is needed now more than ever before. Over the years, I've been careful in many situations to not burn bridges and several recent interactions have benefited me professionally and personally as a result. Who couldn't use that?

I hope that whether you celebrate a birthday in one of the best months or not, this time away from school and all its pressures will allow you to reflect on life's lessons and all that your future has to offer. Enjoy!

REFLECTIONS

Read the below statements and check the ones that apply to you.

○ I have lifelong relationships that are important to me.

○ I can see benefit from all relationships even brief ones.

○ I am not very good at picking my battles.

○ It's easy for me to stay out of other people's business.

○ Kindness is second nature to me.

○ I give to others the same energy they give to me.

Notes:

_____

_____

_____

_____

S.L.O.W. ROAD RULES

CAREGIVER'S CURSE

There are tasks that absolutely need our attention but not EVERY task requires our involvement. Start to watch for ways you can let others help themselves. Sometimes, caring for others means caring enough to let them learn and grow on their own journey.

GROWING UP FROM HERE

None of us wants hard times. However, they are inevitable. Sometimes they come in clusters or spread out over time. The good news is often overcoming one hard time prepares us for the next one. Continue to build that resiliency muscle as you remember your strength and your supports.

GREATER JOY AHEAD

Take a moment to think through your day and pay attention to the things that make you chuckle or smile. It would be easy to say, "the end of the workday" or "bedtime." Focus on those blessings. Look forward with anticipation that more of those moments are coming.

RESET

We may not be able to change everything that needs to be altered, but we can make a difference in some ways. Look for opportunities to influence change within your sphere. You can have a reset in some way. Look for it. Make it happen, even if only for yourself!

REFLECTIONS

It is beneficial to make time to reflect. It helps us to get in touch with ourselves - feelings, thoughts, desires, convictions. Find a time to reflect. Maybe it's on your drive home from work, or while brushing your teeth before bed. Regardless, notice moments when you can think back and plan ahead. It can help!

ONE SELF-LOVE RULE

Write one of your self-love rules.

_____
_____
_____
_____
_____

JULY

As I evaluate my lessons for July, they seem to all have a similar theme. You! It's not too surprising since the purpose of my writing is to share what I'm learning on my self-care journey in hopes it may help you in yours. However, I do find it interesting that in the month that we celebrate our country's independence that perhaps this is a time for you (and me) to also celebrate our individuality.

Not that we don't need other people in our lives; I absolutely believe we do, but it is also good to have our own sense of self. When we know who we are, we have confidence in that being and we celebrate and elevate our own personal goodness. During public speaking engagements, I highlight the value that each of us offers. It can be easy to forget that sometimes. By default, we tend to go straight to the negative. I believe that if we recognize and remember our value, then it is easier for us to prioritize our own wellness. We realize our own worth and are more motivated to protect it. So, let these lessons remind you that you deserve to tell yourself positive stories, take your time, and speak your truth. Use July as a time to not only celebrate America but to also celebrate You!

What Story Are You Telling Yourself?

In the last couple of weeks, I experienced a few different situations and noticed a pattern. Someone (me or somebody else) feels something, reacts to that feeling (under an assumption) and the situation escalates into an energy draining scenario.

One of these situations was with a group of people that I am relatively new to and don't know that well. I am around this group twice a week now and at a recent visit, I got a weird vibe when I walked into the room. It was unusual and the first time I'd felt that with them. I left wondering, "Why don't people here like me?" "What have I done wrong?" It really affected my energy for a couple of hours. A few days later, when I returned, the vibe was completely different, and I felt welcomed and included. I later learned that there had been something going on with one of the employees in the facility during my last visit. Why did I make it about me? It is amazing how we can internalize these experiences without being aware we do that.

As the universe would have it, right as I was in the throes of this realization, I happened to watch a previously taped episode of Super Soul Sunday with Brené Brown. She and Oprah were discussing Brené's newest book, Rising Strong. They were discussing how we can sense something and then tell ourselves a story about what we feel and why, often times, we attribute that feeling to something that may or may not be true. Ding, Ding, Ding! The alarms were going off for me.

Now, I am committed to acknowledging what I'm feeling and exploring where it is coming from. If I'm fabricating a tale or line that I don't know to be true, I need to find out the facts and proceed from there. This approach feels much more freeing. It allows me to feel my feelings, resolve them one way or the other, and move on. I don't have to play and replay tapes, carrying around falsehoods, sometimes for not just hours, but days or years. We all deserve better, to be free from those burdens and have the time and energy to love ourselves and others.

REFLECTIONS

Can you relate to the scenario of telling yourself a story about a situation that may or may not be true? What happened in that situation?

_____
_____
_____
_____
_____
_____
_____
_____

What did you think was happening? What was REALLY happening? What did you learn from that experience?

_____
_____
_____
_____
_____
_____
_____
_____
_____
_____

Time is Your Friend

Another school year has ended, and summer break has begun. Summer is my favorite time of the year. I love how long the days last. I love not having "how's your homework coming?" inquiries. And this year, I've noticed that 8 p.m. in the summer differs greatly from 8 p.m. in the winter. In the summer, at 8 p.m, it's okay to still go to the gym or start a movie or run to the store or even start dinner. In the winter, at 8 p.m. I'd never head to the gym or start a movie; you would find me winding down from the day and getting ready for the next one. It's interesting how different time can feel.

Growing up, my parents raised me to value timeliness, a wiring that can now make me occasionally anxious and irritable. To combat these feelings, I am learning to live S.L.O.W. - Slow down, practice self-care and Wait and Watch for what the universe has in store. I have found that sometimes, situations that cause anxiety can work themselves out. I can't say I have it down yet. I sometimes still default to worry and "control freak" mode, but I'm working on it.

The last month has been a time of testing. Several difficult events unfolded that I was unable to control, making me feel like time was running out. After trying my best, I eventually surrendered. This was not a straightforward process, and several people witnessed my breakdown. Similarly, I have had several other trying times which I've given identifiers such as "the never-ending lice attack of 2003" and "the carpet debacle of 2018." The good news is, as the storm subsides, and I rise out of the rubble, I am stronger and better than when I went in, albeit exhausted.

So, I'm writing about this experience because yet again, I have had to learn that time is my friend. There is so much to gain by letting go, waiting and watching, and allowing space and time to work things out. It is less draining emotionally, physically, and mentally to give up worry or control, especially with things you can't control. Will you join me so that together, we can continue to practice living a life of peace and regularly welcome our friend, time to the table?

REFLECTIONS

THINK OF A TIME WHEN YOU WANTED SOMETHING DESPERATELY AND HAD TO WAIT FOR IT. HOW WERE YOU DURING THAT WAITING PERIOD?

A. ANXIOUS
B. CAREFREE
C. EXCITED
D   OTHER_____

DID YOUR DEMEANOR IMPACT THE OUTCOME/TIMEFRAME?

A. YES
B. SOMEWHAT
C. NO
D   OTHER_____

DID YOUR DEMEANOR IMPACT YOU, YOUR HEALTH, OTHERS?

A. YES
B. SOMEWHAT
C. NO
D   OTHER_____

WAS IT WORTH IT?

A. YES
B. SOMEWHAT
C. NO
D   OTHER_____

Are You There Yet?

It's July and I have a few questions: How are you doing? Have you found your slower pace? Have you begun to unplug and relax? Are you there yet? If you are anything like me, it takes some time to switch gears from going full force during the workday to embracing a break. If you aren't careful, these couple of months can be easily overrun with graduation parties, camps, trips, visits from family and friends and potentially appointments no one had time for during the school year.

Typically, everyone takes at least one vacation over the summer. There have been many times I've come back from a vacation feeling like I needed another vacation, especially if you have small kids. Consider ways to safeguard some time for yourself to refresh. What are the things you enjoy doing that feed your soul/spirit? What helps to rejuvenate you?

It's also possible during these months off, you have friends and family who, knowing you have "more time" available, have numerous ideas of ways you can fill up that extra space with things they want or need. However, it is ok to establish boundaries and to assert yourself to ensure you are taking care of you. I did that recently and initially I felt guilty about limiting my availability at a friend's event, but she didn't mind that I left, and I felt good about having the energy to do other necessary things.

I hope that before the summer flies by, which it always does, we will intentionally plan time to do things that rejuvenate us. Can you set aside time in the mornings before the day gets going to do some reflection or meditation? Can you build in time for a nap during the day or take a walk or meet up with friends? Whatever feeds your soul, figure that out and prioritize it for yourself. And hopefully before too long we will be in the habit of going S.L.O.W., looking out for our own wellness and we won't have to keep asking, "Are we there yet?"

REFLECTIONS

1) What is an area of self-care you've grown in recently?

2)How do you safeguard yourself, your energy, your time, your wellness?

3)How do you ensure you would make it to your goal?

4) Do you have a new destination and a plan to get there? If so, how?

Speak Your Truth

These last several years - with the protests and the commitment to change racial inequality, social injustice, and police brutality - have moved me. It has been heartbreaking to see the loss of life, to hear the stories and experiences of so many and it's been humbling to do my own reading, soul-searching, and reflecting on ways I have contributed to this societal norm, even if inadvertently. I've had to wrestle with my truth and find the courage to speak it out loud to others. I've had to communicate what does and doesn't work for me. Being vulnerable is hard. Being honest about my thoughts and feelings in personal and professional settings can feel awkward.

For years, my goal was to be "Happy and Free." When I'm not in this space, I feel uneasy and unsettled. Many people share this experience, feeling stuck and unaware. However, you/we have the power to ensure our happiness and freedom. Speak your truth and have those crucial conversations. Share your perspective and stand for your values and plan for yourself, as you have equal value and importance.

Because I'm still learning how to speak my truth, depending on the intensity of the situation, I sometimes have to practice. My family laughs at me, but I have even been known to use note cards. This technique gives me strength and courage to use my voice. If it was significant enough to write down, it also needs to be said.

When I'm in my car, I sometimes listen to stand-up comedians depending on my mood and what I need at that time. I heard a comedian tell a joke about his pledge to live by the 10 Commandments. He shared that he is committed to "not telling falsehoods" and always being honest. His set was hilarious, but truth be told, being honest is hard! It takes courage, whether you are one person in a large group of people who all share your view, or if you are alone, with coworkers, your boss, or your family and friends, standing up for yourself. This summer and beyond, speaking your truth for you is necessary and worth it so that you, too, can be happy and free!

REFLECTIONS

Read the below statements and check the ones that apply to you.

- ⬤ I find it easy to be open about my convictions.

- ⬤ I understand and embrace what it means to speak my truth.

- ⬤ I speak my truth only to people I trust.

- ⬤ I speak my truth to anyone who asks.

- ⬤ I am open to learning from others who challenge what I believe or think.

- ⬤ I am not open to changing my way of thinking.

Notes:
_____
_____
_____
_____

Making Lemonade

As a young child, I frequently got earaches. Often during the summer months, it was swimmer's ear since I lived in the pool in our neighborhood. I vividly remember one day sitting on the back patio after a day of swimming, drinking lemonade. Each time I would swallow, my ear would pop and ached. In my young mind, I equated lemonade with earaches. For YEARS after that, when people asked me if I wanted lemonade, I told them "no" saying I was allergic to it and that it gave me ear infections. People would give me a strange look, but it didn't really register with me because I was convinced drinking lemonade lead to my earaches. As embarrassing as it is to admit this, it wasn't until much later, like into my young adulthood, that I realized the ridiculousness of that belief and have enjoyed lemonade since pain free. And in fact, its's one of my favorite drinks, I crave it, especially on warm summer days.

Perhaps because of my love of lemonade, I frequently use the saying "When life gives you lemons, make lemonade." To say we have had to make lemonade over the last few years is an understatement. I can't think of anyone who hasn't had some type of challenge to overcome during these unprecedented times.

I took part in a project recently that provided school administrators a space to talk about their resilience through these times. My colleagues and I convened several focus groups of school leaders across the state, asking them to identify the things that went well since the pandemic and social justice occurrences. It would be so easy to only talk about all the difficulties and challenges, but we intentionally wanted to look at the bright side and ways they were proactive. It was uplifting and inspiring to hear and learn from them, their humility, intentionality, and determination.

As we revel in some downtime during the summer break, I hope we continue to build the resilience muscle we've been conditioning and hat we hold on to the good that we've created. Remember, there are silver linings and kick back friends, and enjoy your fresh made lemonade this summer.

REFLECTIONS

Think about a time you were disappointed. Perhaps someone let you down. Or as is typical with COVID, something had to cancel or be adjusted. How did you respond in that situation?

_____
_____
_____
_____
_____
_____
_____
_____

Did you let yourself feel your feelings? Were you then able to regroup, reframe, and "make lemonade?" How did it play out? Did it work out satisfactorily?

_____
_____
_____
_____
_____
_____
_____
_____
_____
_____
_____

S.L.O.W. ROAD RULES

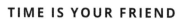

WHAT STORY ARE YOU TELLING YOURSELF?

Pay attention to the lines you feed yourself about your own situation or other people's. It's ok to ask for clarification if you can't let it go (rather than burning your energy spinning tales) because you know what they say about assuming.

TIME IS YOUR FRIEND

It is hard to be patient. It's hard to see "on the other side" sometimes. But it is there. The universe knows better than us. Trust it. It will not disappoint, even if it's not until later. Wait and Watch.

ARE YOU THERE YET?

Find someone in your circle who is also on a self-care journey. Share this self-care victory with them. Give them the details. Learn about their journey. Swap stories, just like you would about a vacation. Encourage each other to keep going to your next stop. Road trips are more fun with friends.

SPEAK YOUR TRUTH

It can be scary and vulnerable to vocalize your beliefs and the things that make you,well, you. Finding ways to communicate with kindness and conviction takes practice, especially if you feel like your voice isn't being heard or validated. It's okay to start small. Test the waters and build your confidence one statement at a time.

MAKING LEMONADE

It's tough when things don't go the way we want. Sometimes it works out even better and sometimes it just is what it is, and we have to learn to be okay with it. Either way, it's less draining if we just surrender and let things be what they will be, even if we don't like it.

ONE SELF-LOVE RULE

Write one of your self-love rules.

QUARTERLY REVIEW

MAY- JULY

BABY STEPS I TOOK

1 _____
2 _____
3 _____

PROUDEST MOMENTS

1 _____
2 _____
3 _____

HIGHLIGHTS

_____
_____

LESSONS I LEARNED

_____
_____

WHAT WORKED

_____
_____
_____
_____
_____
_____

DO BETTER NEXT TIME

_____
_____
_____
_____
_____
_____

IMPROVEMENTS TO MAKE

_____
_____
_____
_____

CONCLUSION

Working on this compendium provided many opportunities for me to reflect on my own self-care. As they say, you teach what you need to learn. It definitely has been a journey, which is obvious as you read through the blogs, month by month, year by year.

You can see the evolution of my practice. I have grown in my self-awareness and in finding the courage to speak up and say what I need. It isn't always easy, but it is always worth it. I've also gotten better at setting boundaries, knowing what I'm okay with and what doesn't work for me. I gauge how I'm going to spend my energy by asking: What are my priorities? Where do my values lie? What will have the greatest impact? And finally, the overall area of growth is practicing what I preach, slowing down and being more intentional.

It's hard to teach this old dog new tricks, but it helps, as I have experienced the benefits of pacing myself and letting things work themselves out. It alleviates the need to be in control, the worrying, and all the stress. It's so freeing. These are the same strategies I encourage others to implement.

Life has a funny way of ensuring we learn those important lessons. Times of testing present themselves as opportunities to strengthen that self-care muscle. With each victory or step forward, you prove to yourself you can do it. Or, as my mom says, you build your personal resume. And like with most things, the more you do it, the easier it becomes. Then you can realize your own evolution. Thank you for going on this journey with me. Hopefully, in time, for all of us, it will become second nature.

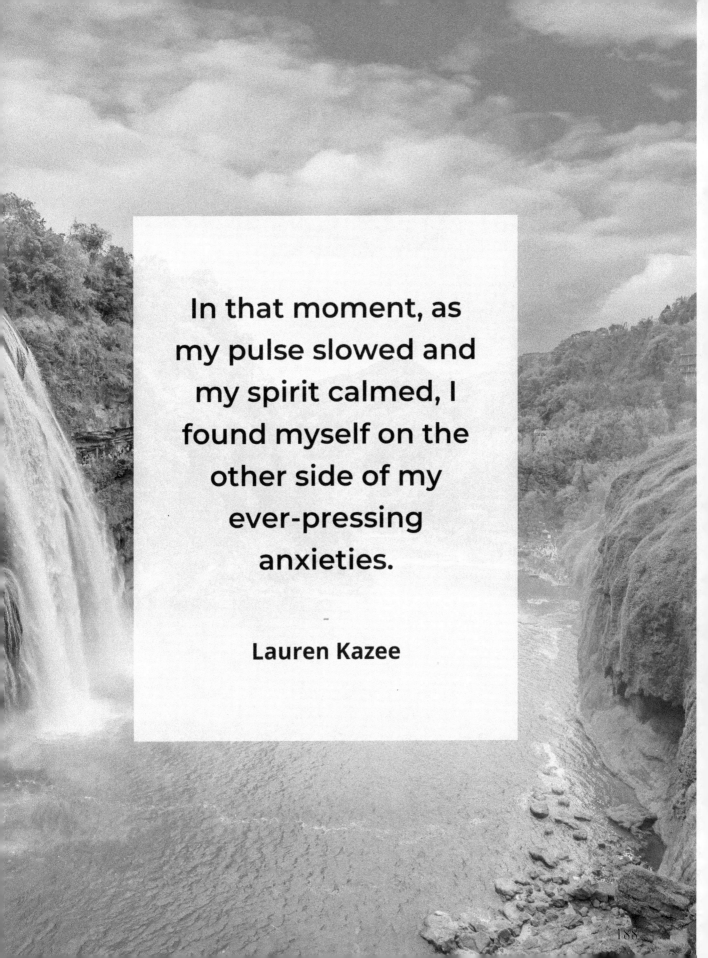

In that moment, as my pulse slowed and my spirit calmed, I found myself on the other side of my ever-pressing anxieties.

Lauren Kazee

NOTES

NOTES

NOTES

NOTES

RESOURCE LIBRARY

LIVING S.L.O.W.

Educator support groups, workshops, consultations, and coaching are just some of the treats found at the Living Slow website. Visit www.livingslow.org to learn how to take your self-care to the next level.

CREATE

The CREATE for Education hosts the CARE program which provides professional development for educators. Visit www.createforeducation.org.

PURE EDGE

Pure Edge, Inc. provides resources to educators and students to help them be more mindful and well. You can visit them at www.pureedgeinc.org.

MORE INFO

WWW.LIVINGSLOW.ORG

SIGN UP AND BE THE FIRST TO KNOW
WHEN THERE'S A WORKSHOP IN YOUR AREA

Lauren Kazee conducts workshops for educators year-round. Visit her website a full version of each lesson by title. You can also sign up to receive self-care tips and updates on workshops, seminars, and conferences that may be coming to your school district.

THANK YOU!

I have a deep respect for educators, caregivers, and professionals living a life of service. Thank you for allowing me to contribute to your self-care journey through your purchase of this workbook.

If you would like to connect with me or offer feedback on how this workbook has helped you, please visit my website below.

WWW.LIVINGSLOW.ORG

Printed in the USA
CPSIA information can be obtained
at www.ICGtesting.com
CBHW082257080224
4132CB00002B/10

9 780980 115925